In this gorgeous collection of poetry, Scheponik brings an artist's eye, a believer's faith, and a poet's sensibilities to work that both illuminates and celebrates life in all its joys and complications. We are drawn into the beauty of the places Scheponik creates for us through careful observation and lyrical expression. We find ourselves experiencing the poet's wonder at the natural world and his joyous faith that is rooted in the beauty of the things of that world. We see ourselves in these poems, which use imagery from particular moments to build a landscape in which those moments become universal expressions of human experience, and we relate deeply to Scheponik's exploration of what it means to be a parent, a child, a lover, a friend. You will find yourself returning to these poems again and again, and each time you will find they offer something new to engage and enlighten you.

—Wendy Galgan,
published poet and editor of *Assisi:
An Online Journal of Arts & Letters*

From the first time Dr. Peter Scheponik's poetry arrived in my editor's inbox, it was clear this was standout material in a league with the best I've read in all the years I've been publishing literary magazines. I would describe this book as "reflections of a life thoughtfully lived." Three of my favorite pieces: "I Heard a Spider Singing, "Considering My Grandsons," and "The Echo of God Tears." Nature, family, and God's Universe. What more is there?

—Nadia Giordana,
publisher, executive editor, *WINK:
Writers in the Know* magazine

In *Seeing, Believing, and Other Things*, P.C. Scheponik employs eager pen and abundant heart to explore the sublime interstices of quotidian existence. Whether pausing over the beautiful brutality that makes us sigh the moment the truth bleeds into consciousness or losing himself—and us, his readers, along with him—amidst the helixed emptiness that all living species share, the poet approaches not only the world but the universe at large with a curious blend of wide-eyed wonder and world-weary experience. Evoking shades of Whitman, Scheponik's poetic eye spots the divine majesty in all of creation as he sings of the delicate balance between life and death with joy and reverence. Here is a poet with humor and heart, at home among the silken protein notes of a spider web as he is partaking in the beautiful dance of the galaxy across the field of infinity. His poems are self-described love letters to God, family, and all of creation, and although—spoiler alert—everything falls to pieces in the end, we are fortunate to have the poetry in this collection to shine a light on all that is beautiful and wondrous in our universe until then.

—Marc Schuster,
author of *The Grievers* and *Tired of California*,
editor of *Small Press Reviews*

SEEING, BELIEVING, AND OTHER THINGS

Seeing, Believing, and Other Things

A collection of poems

by

P.C. SCHEPONIK

Adelaide Books
New York / Lisbon
2021

SEEING, BELIEVING, AND OTHER THINGS
A collection of poems
By P.C. Scheponik

Copyright © by P.C. Scheponik
Cover design © 2021 Adelaide Books
Cover Art by Melissa Diliberto

Published by Adelaide Books, New York / Lisbon
adelaidebooks.org

Editor-in-Chief
Stevan V. Nikolic

All rights reserved. No part of this book may be reproduced in any manner whatsoever without written permission from the author except in the case of brief quotations embodied in critical articles and reviews.

For any information, please address Adelaide Books
at info@adelaidebooks.org
or write to:
Adelaide Books
244 Fifth Ave. Suite D27
New York, NY, 10001

ISBN: 978-1-954351-96-7

Printed in the United States of America

To my wife Shirley, the love of my life, whose compassion, strength, and single-hearted love encouraged me be me.

Special Thanks

To Stevan Nikolic for his deep commitment to and love for poetry and his support, promotion, and editorial expertise, which made the publication of this book possible.

Contents

Acknowledgements **19**

SEEING

Form and Content *23*

Daybreak *24*

Forever *25*

Moment of Truth *26*

The End Is Song *27*

Fog Rolls In *29*

Ode to Sparrows *30*

Cardinal's Bath *31*

Regal Red Tailed *32*

In Heaven's Name *33*

Cardinal in a Sycamore Tree *34*

Sparrow Song *35*

From a Distance *36*

Trinity *37*

The Edge *38*

On Any Terms *39*

Life Conquers All *40*

World Afraid of Dying *41*

The Difference *43*

The Magic in Motion *45*

Desert Starfire *46*

Wild Wind *47*

Ode to Seasons *48*

The Indispensability of Light *50*

Chime Song on a Winter Night *51*

January's Secret *52*

Dawn *53*

Of Beauty's Love *54*

Stones *55*

Love Reverberates *56*

On Seeing the Painting of Pear and Peach *57*

Two Squirrels Dancing *58*

Lessons Learned *60*

Poem for My Age Spots *62*

SEEING, BELIEVING, AND OTHER THINGS

Waking in the Dream *63*

Beauty's Touch *64*

Expectation *65*

When Dragonflies Dance *66*

I Heard a Spider Singing *67*

Ode to a Dead Cricket *68*

By a Thread *69*

Things Ants Taught Me *70*

Chasing the Sun *71*

A Spider's Life *72*

Love Requited *74*

Gnat Fest *75*

Considering My Grandsons *76*

BELIEVING

Pond Song *79*

Love Is in the Proof *80*

This Moment of Truth *81*

Stardust *83*

When Matter Sings *84*

Truth and Belief *85*

Walking Toward a Vision of Truth *86*

Love Story *87*

The Echo of God Tears *89*

The Devil in Us *90*

Fair Share *91*

Coming Storm *92*

Never Ending *93*

Love Letters *94*

Words *95*

Love Child, That Time Before Morning *96*

In a Grain of Sand *98*

Amber and Rust *100*

True Story *101*

Stepping into Love Time *102*

When Stars Fall *103*

Wordburst *105*

Only the Lost Can See *106*

Star Love *107*

The Coming God Hour *108*

My Youngest Brother Calls Me *110*

Because *112*

Maybe *113*

No Match for the Heart on Fire *114*

SEEING, BELIEVING, AND OTHER THINGS

Tides of Grace *116*

White Anglers *117*

Goodwill News *118*

Morning Prayer *119*

Night Song *120*

The Flowers Give *121*

The Imprint *122*

The Longing *123*

An Easter Morn of Sorts *124*

Things Made *125*

Psalm *126*

Losing Myself *127*

Oceanus Hymn *128*

The Making *129*

OTHER THINGS

The Sorrow and the Shame *133*

What of Forever *134*

There Comes a Point *135*

Learning to Read at 63 *136*

Of Promises and Keeping *137*

Last Chapter *138*

Things of This World   *139*

Time's Promise   *140*

The Understanding   *141*

For the Woman Crying at Kohl's   *142*

The Need   *144*

Book of Life   *146*

The Fear   *147*

In Comparison   *148*

Something Important   *150*

Eleventh Grade English (For Peter Doyle)   *151*

Oh Night, My Friend   *152*

My Place in the Family of Things   *153*

The Art of the Poem   *154*

No Surprise to the Stars   *155*

And what of Poetry   *157*

Universe of Words   *159*

Word Shine   *160*

Reclamation   *161*

For the Love of God   *162*

Second Chances   *163*

Night Talk   *164*

Who Loves the Poet?   *165*

"What Can I do?" *167*

For Love of Women *168*

Sexual Persuasions *170*

Choice Is a Solemn Matter *172*

Underdog *174*

Ascension *175*

Old Men and Their Dogs *176*

Poem Almost Never Written *178*

Butterfly Boy *179*

The Past Cannot Live Up to Itself *180*

Poet *181*

Pain Deep *182*

Love's Tabernacle *183*

Youth's Season *184*

What to Say (For Heather Harris) *185*

Loving My Father *187*

The Grieving *189*

Efficiency *191*

Blame Game *193*

About the Author *195*

Acknowledgements

Deep gratitude and acknowledgement is expressed to the editors and publishers of the journals that first published some of the poems in this collection.

Adelaide Independent Quarterly Literary Magazine: "The End Is Song," "I Thought," "Love Is in the Proof," and "Pond Song."

All the Sins: "The Magic in the Motion."

Assisi: An Online Journal of Arts and Letters: "When Matter Sings" and "The Sorrow and the Shame."

Badlands Literary Journal: "Gnat Fest."

Big Windows Review: "Chasing the Sun."

Boned: A Collection of Skeletal Writing: "What of Forever," "Daybreak," and "There Comes a Point."

Del Sol Review: "Learning to Read at 63" and "Of Promises and Keeping."

Grey Sparrow Journal: "The End Is Song."

North of Oxford: "Truth and Belief."

Ottawa Arts Review: "Last Chapter," " Things of This World," and "Time's Promise."

Peeking Cat Poetry Magazine: "Trinity."

The Phoenix: "The Edge" and "Something Important."

Poetry Pacific: "Sparrow Song" and "Understanding."

Red Eft Review: "For the Woman Crying at Kohl's" and "The Need."

Sincerely Magazine: "The Book of Life."

Smoky Blue Literary and Arts Magazine: "The Fear."

Time of Singing Literary Magazine: "Fog Rolls In."

The Visitant: "Eleventh Grade English: For Peter Doyle."

Westward Quarterly: "Oh Night, My Friend."

The Wire's Dream Magazine: "From a Distance" and "In Comparison."

Writers in the Know (WINK): "Beauty's Touch," "Cardinal in Sycamore Tree," "Things Ants Taught me," "Expectation," "Form and Content," "In Heaven's Name," "My Place in the Family of Things," and "Moment of Truth."

SEEING

Form and Content

They descended suddenly, an apparition landing on the lake,
a dozen Canadian geese touching down,
great wings curving, cupping the air,
creating rings that shirred the lake's mirrored surface.
As each goose touched one webbed foot to water,
each became a pair—a bird and its reflection,
toe-tip to toe-tip, miming each other in the sun's glare
as they landed on the lake, tucked their wings into their sides,
shimmied their tails and began to
glide across the surface shine.
It was like seeing the realm of Platonic ideals realized,
the secrets of cosmologic design taking me by storm,
in that moment the geese landed, in that moment I saw form
and content become one for the very first time.

Daybreak

The morning wind combs willow's hair,
strand by weeping strand.
Trembling silver edges, teeth made of air
slide softly through the green-leaf mane
with a mother's love or a lover's care.
All is peace and gentleness.
Sun's golden hands softly caress
the edges of glowing clouds.
Heaven's blue cheek is brightly rouged
with dawn's blush, and drowsing moon,
a bit confused, seems in a rush to clothe
her pale nakedness with an indigo robe of sky.
While robin sings a matin song and starlings fly
in black star throngs to celebrate the break of day.
My heart rises with each note, and my soul longs
to find its way deep into the beauty this world shows,
into the perfect truth the body knows when it's
seduced by morning.

Forever

The sumac is blood red
and beaten gold illumination
in November's morning breath,
cold translation of life to death.
These leafy lumens, a welcome change
to the sky's dreary, sullen, grey face.
This is a change that seems to say
in clouded words, "Today is the day,
the season of Demeter's wrath.
Winter cometh and all life
must pass away."
So gather the color and the light
you find among every leaf and limb.
Store up the glories of autumn's sights.
Enjoy the poignancy of their dying hymns:
songs to beauty, songs to truth,
songs of joy and the will to live
in love with life forever.

Moment of Truth

I remember it so clearly—
the morning, the lawn, the red-tailed hawk,
the mourning dove in the hawk's sharp, red talons,
the tufts of dove down clinging to the blades of grass
like an erasure smear from the side of death's hand,
brushing the debris from life's page.
I remember the fierce look in the raptor's eyes—
piercing determination to take its share of nourishment.
I don't know if the hawk partook its breakfast on the lawn,
or if the winged carnivore spirited the dove's corpse to
some limb in a tall tree or to the top of a pole from a
telephone line to devour its fill of pleasure, to obey
the mandate to survive.
I know there are laws in this world, written in the blood
that flows through our veins, savage statutes that allow
us to thrive at the expense of other lives—
a beautiful brutality that makes us sigh
that moment the truth bleeds through.

The End Is Song

Walking the dog this morning,
I came upon a dragonfly
lying on the concrete walk,
on its back, legs, in slow motion,
treading air.
Though it seemed like it wanted
to turn over and fly,
the earthbound aviator remained
there on the ground.
It was a young dragon,
whose cellophane wings were
so clear they seemed to disappear
against the rough face of pavement.
The insect was dying.
The precise deliberation of its passing
pressed into my mind.
I know in the great scheme of life,
the death of a single dragonfly
doesn't seem like much.
But watching this creature
release itself—
or watching it being released
from this world,
touched something very deep
in me.
As if fate had led me to this place,

as if earth whispered in a voice
made of grace delicate as a
dragonfly's wing:
Look and see.
This is how it is done.
This is how you sing the end.

Fog Rolls In

The fog padded softly in,
curled around the beach,
her cool grey fur
blanketing the shore
in luxuriant coat.
I felt like I was walking
through a cloud,
a starless, moonless, almost night,
a hazy shroud of dying light of day.
The fog rolled and rubbed,
stretched out on her smoky side
and brushed damp paws against my coat
as if to play some cat and mouse game.
But I couldn't stay.
Night was on its way, and I had to be on mine.
So I bid the fog adieu, thanked her for her time.
And as I turned and walked away,
felt her purring nonchalance
rubbing in soft memory
against the legs of my mind.

Ode to Sparrows

The sparrows' voices break the sultry calm of July morn,
chirping the same song, the one I heard as a boy on those
hot summer days walking through the cool pools of shade
the sycamore leaves made on the city streets.
The soles of my feet careful not to step on the crack
that might break my mother's back.
The countless ants scurrying in and out among the weeds
that grew in the lifts and fissures of
concrete that couldn't keep
mother nature away, but heaved and broke, forced to obey
the truth that you cannot yolk nature's power to human will.
The sparrows are singing this summer morning,
and the boy's heart rises in this old man's soul, still willing
to listen to their song.

Cardinal's Bath

Cardinal in his scarlet garb
takes the time to preen and bathe.
Dips beneath the crystal pool.
Flings the water with his wings
till his feathers are bejeweled,
fully studded, diamond bright,
an elegance of water and light.
Shimmies his tail
and thrashes his wings.
Then in voice triumphant sings.
Leaps from the water
and flies away.
Cardinal is beauty, bath, and play.

Regal Red Tailed

He sits, solitary watcher
on the telephone wire.
A young red-tailed hawk,
a crown prince surveying
his future kingdom.
His stature, puffed
in February's chill.
His feathers,
royal cape draped
about the shoulders
of his folded wings.
This would-be ascendant,
future king of sky and field.
This warrior raptor
whose beak and talons
whose vision and wings
will make small earthbound
animals yield to shadows and fears.
He holds court there
on the lonely station of an otherwise
empty telephone wire—
a force to be reckoned with,
a primal desire to survive,
to rule with the urgency
of wings spread wide enough
to block out the sun for anyone in his path.

In Heaven's Name

The sparrows are up early this morning,
milling about the macadam road—
obviously searching for something to eat,
some wayward insect, some wind-blown seed.
The street is filled with their petit dejeuner chatter—
Who will be first to find the early worm?
Who will bathe in last night's puddle,
lying alongside the curb?
They hop, and chirp, and flutter.
I notice as they rise, there are others—
darker versions of themselves, following their every move,
a flock of shadow mimes that prove everyone has a double.
I find this both miracle and mystery, this
morning sparrow world,
such majesty in the moment.
How shall I do justice to it? What shall I name it?
I know; I'll call it heaven.

Cardinal in a Sycamore Tree

A cardinal landed on a sycamore branch,
a dream of feathers the color of blood,
sat there amid the rain-soaked leaves
shivering tears that fell each time the
late September breeze embraced
the sycamore's slick bark arms.
I watched this prince of birds hold court
with wind and rain and leaves,
cock, to one side, his mitred head,
then, as if pleased with his sanguine grace,
flared his tail and both wings spread,
and with the ease of a word well said,
this living dream made the leaves bleed
as he flew away.

Sparrow Song

A trinity of sparrows came to me
while I was sitting beneath an oak tree
at a weathered picnic table in the park,
a placid place where I am able
to seek the words that would express
my soul's deep longing for the caress
of God's own hand upon its face—
the touch of truth, the feel of grace
loosed in me in bountiful ways.
The perfect moment, time and space
suspended,
as if to wait for beauty and truth to be
blended—
the words to be born—
the meanings bud, the sounds form
their dream petals deep inside.
The way the yolk within the egg resides,
a golden sun that silently hides
'til it clothes itself in the promise of
feathers, in the purpose of song.
Then breaks free from the shell
to enter the world where it belongs,
for a time to fly, for a time to sing,
like these tiny sparrows so close to me.
I could almost touch; I could almost reach
the truth in their sweet song.

From a Distance

The gulls come every morning to the
place I spread the pieces of bread.
They arrive like angels, lowering through
the air, wings in arcs, webbed feet
dropped as if touching land was a divine
dare, to step out of grace and into
this world, prepared to taste its goodness.
The gulls twitch their wings, lock
them in place. Then, begins the Darwinian
race, as hungry beaks jab at the feed.
Heads thrust back, feathered breasts heave
in celebration of their right to eat,
followed by anguished cries and wings
that beat the air with urgency.
Calling, calling, painfully until the famished
others arrive. White-feathered
throngs of hunger, descending from the
sky. Then the breast-butting and
wing-thrashing begins. The battle cries
intensify, and competition wins.
Driven by the hidden imperative to
survive, wings rise and fall
like feathered swords as frenzied gulls
seize their rewards, rushing one
another and beating each other away. From
a distance, war can look a lot
like play—but only from a distance.

Trinity

Waves, silver with sunlight,
glossy with diamond shine,
lunge in mercurial passion
exploding in salt-foam fashion
as they race along the wind-tossed
coast.

Sky, blue bowl of emptiness,
arches in a vaulting dome
that captures ocean's urgency,
claims the shell-strewn beach
as its own.

Wind, ancient Titan, wildly blows.
The whole world bows beneath his breath
in a truth that knows no bounds.

The Edge

I am drawn to the shore—
always have been,
a coastal dweller
living along the edges
of life
of love
of things—
willing to enter,
deep, not too deep,
fearful of the songs
darkness sings,
songs of being swallowed whole,
separated from the light,
from the sky—
being owned by the night
that never lets go.
I like to walk along the shoreline,
following the tides,
listening to the surf's alluring roll.
But it is the edge, the line, the thin
tightrope I claim as mine,
that delicate balance between
risk and control that beckons me
to step ever so carefully—
one foot at a time—
lured by the roar, by the endless roll
of the sea of universe rushing toward
the shores of the sublime.

On Any Terms

Three gulls huddle in the sand,
feather-puff breasts,
pressed by November's gusting breath
as she draws her sea-green arms
in white rushes of salt-foam waves,
tumbles of stone shards,
moonshells and clams,
swirling revolutions splayed
across countless grains of sand,
the beach's tear-stained face
that spans the stretch of grace
as far as eyes can yield to light and place.
So much of earth's perfection,
such loveliness and affection given—
free of charge—
this world, this life at large for the taking
by you, by me on any terms
by which our wandering hearts are driven—
on any terms.

Life Conquers All

The beach this morning is a battleground scene.
The hulls of countless horseshoe crabs,
strewn like helmets of the dead,
the brave who soldiered on,
despite the surf's relentless tread,
clashing below the crashing waves,
finally falling prey to death—
the sharp beaks of the ravenous gulls
lancing, piercing amidst the swells
of whitecaps thundering against the shore.
These many dead who have procured
these many living who take their stand,
full-bellied, wings folded, web-footed
upon the sand.
Feather-breasted in the wind
till battle cry from fierce throat rings
and the sky is alive with the song that sings:
Life conquers all.

World Afraid of Dying

Three sugar maple leaves
run along the beach
in a twirl-wind tumble
from tip to tip,
soft rustle in morning air,
crisp nimble spinning
without a care.
There is a freedom—
a life left behind
of branch-root connections
holding on to shade,
to color, to transubstantiated
sugar of light,
the earth's garden green,
turned to gold that
finally bleeds sunset beauty.
The truth of autumn's duty,
to take back all that
summer has to give,
to whisper the secrets
of snow and silence,
the chance to live again—
after the ice and winter moon
have their time to pretend
the world belongs to them.
Three leaves running

P.C. Scheponik

along the beach,
carrying the world
within their parchment palms,
like a sacred lesson,
a truth too perfect to teach
a world afraid of dying.

The Difference

I spotted it lying there at the foam-
lipped edge of a retreating wave,
a cream-colored whelk, full and beautiful,
still glistening with the kiss
of salt water and sun. I rushed over in
thrill, in awe, to be the one to
receive such a gift from the sea. On reaching
down and lifting the whelk up,
I could feel a heaviness deeply cupped in
the tabernacle shell. I turned it over
to dispel both sea water and sand, but the
whelk shell was filled with a living
being that moved as I ran my hand across
its suctioned hold. The pod of the
mollusk, determined and controlled, hunkered
down in refusal to ever let go.
When I took the edge in my fingertips and
gingerly tugged, the creature retracted,
and silently shrugged, shrinking back
into the shell's marble throat.
As if to flee the shock of my touch—the feel
of first assault, as if the fear of death
was too much for it to bear. I sensed the
helixed emptiness that all living species
share. I felt the victim cringe, part determination
to survive, part fear. I felt it tighten

its grip on its life, here, on this earth— its need
to go on. And with the full strength of
my right arm, I tossed the whelk back into the
sea. It dropped with a small gulp, into
the deep Atlantic green, a hope, an escape, an
altered destiny. I stood there and thought,
or maybe I prayed that this whelk I released
would find a safe way to the ocean floor,
bury itself beneath the sand, draw in the plankton,
the water, the salt, the dark nutrients
that dwelled in earth's deepest flesh and live a
full life, without the threat of gull's beak
or human hand. And after its long life came to
an end, after the lump of its living soul
became mattery bits and slipped in silence between
grains of sand, I prayed the white-shell
temple of its body might wash ashore again, and
that I might stand before its mollusk memory,
a living man, and that I might lift it, once more, in
gentle hands, and celebrate the eternal plan
connecting two who loved this world, deeply
enough to know when to hold on, when let go,
and to understand the difference.

The Magic in Motion

The sandpiper runs
as if its life depends upon
moving faster than
the lacey-edged tongues
of surf.
How the piper's legs move
like pistons that prove
the power of locomotion.
How the white caps swell
as if compelled
by some secret magic
of the ocean.
It almost seems
movement is God
and all things dreams
of action.
The tides come,
and the tides go.
The beach is sacrificed
to their traction.
I see what I see.
I know what I know—
this dance of living power.
The smaller I get,
the larger I grow,
as the seconds turn into hours.

Desert Starfire

Her sand and rocks, kissed red by late-day sun,
call to my tumbleweed heart that runs in wild abandon
toward the sky that bleeds beauty across the horizon
soaking the clouds in time's red truth.
I see the evening star rise, diamond solitaire,
set below a slice of marble moon, sidled there,
like a Mona Lisa smile, knowing more than she'll ever tell
of love, of longing, of living forever in a tear shed by God
before light took its very first breath.
Darkness has its secrets, the sight we
seek in desert sands and stars,
in clouds who keep their distance drifting
only as far as destiny allows.
These dreams we share as we cast up our eyes, send forth our
sojourning hearts, like wishes, like
prayers to someone listening,
someone who hears our deepest
desires, to someone who cares
for the starfire that burns in all of us.

Wild Wind

The wind tonight is wild.
Gusting, per hour, more than 40 miles.
An invisible sea, heaving great waves
over balconies and through the streets.
Sweeping trash cans and newspapers,
Styrofoam cups, plastic bottles, and leaves
in a fury of tumbling, dancing debris
in dervish swirls that fill my heart
with an ecstasy that tastes like power,
feels like release, as if I could be
one of those cups or bottles,
or rumble-bumble cans.
Nature is so potent, so free,
and the imagination, such a tease telling me,
"Open the door. Let yourself be taken,
swallowed by the uncontrolled harlotry.
Go body! Go mind! Go soul!
Headlong in the rush toward the unknown.
Swept up in the moment the world explodes
in ways you couldn't conceive,
in dreams you wouldn't dare believe
could possibly be your own.

Ode to Seasons

The leftover leaves in late November on oleander arms
form orange-tipped tears pressed between
the invisible pages of time.
The way flower petals are laid to rest
between smooth vellum edges
of those paper tongues that whisper secrets
between the bindings of books—
narratives of lives transubstantiated into words,
the way the bread becomes the body, the
way the wine becomes the blood,
the way they both become the small, tasteless
wafer placed upon the tongue.
The way the disc begins to unravel, slowly
dissolve into pasty pulp,
matter returning to its unassembled state.
Tale told, experience digested the way the last
leaves will fall, shed like tiny sorrows.
And the earth will open its wet-loam lips
and swallow the last of those leaves
who will silently slip like dark secrets down
darker throats to steam and slough,
to form the dark notes of nutrients' song.
When the days are short, when the nights
are long, and Persephone dreams
of being reborn.
Till the earth strings together a root-hair score.

SEEING, BELIEVING, AND OTHER THINGS

Then the trees will trumpet, and the bushes blare.
Then the flowers will sing for joy in April's baptismal air,
in praise of maternity as Demeter bares her breasts
and nurses the earth in tenderness
from her milky fonts of love.

The Indispensability of Light

The evening fog has made the moon a blurred, golden smile.
The evening star, a tear-filled eye, glistens vibrantly, about
to cry for sorrow or for joy.
The night is anyone's guess—yielding girl, satisfied boy,
the tenderness, the careful ploys of love that bring the roof
down.
Moon and stars, the planet turning round and round,
grinding truth against beauty, leaving scars too deep
to be removed.
Leaving misty memories of the fragile moods of love
that wax and wane and conclude in darkness
that ruins but ultimately proves the indispensability
of light.

Chime Song on a Winter Night

The chimes call in winter wind.
Their song, the color of stars.
Flames pulsing, icy bright.
White whims sprawled across the sky.
Splattering astral majesty,
flung in patterned flicks.
As if God took His favorite brush,
dipped it in His deepest love,
then driven in a frenzied rush—
fire made of pure desire—
decorated dead of night
with precious dreams of day.
Oh, beautiful dance of galaxy
across the field of infinity,
creating a quantum way
in bold God-strokes.
This vision of reality
bends time and space infallibly
into hope that burns like faith,
that tastes like love upon the tongue,
that makes me kneel before the night,
that draws me to the sacred song sung
by chimes in notes as bright and beautiful
as stars on a winter night.

January's Secret

Oh January, with your snow-white sky
and silver sea, take me into your winter arms,
and share your stoic mystery.
The beauty of your ice-born tears.
The glory of your boundless snow.
Take me, January, to your frozen breast.
Suckle me until I know the fullness of your loveliness,
the truth behind the winds that blow
their cold across the earth,
that put the world to sleep.
Let me, January, into your heart,
slip into your dreams where need conspires
to meet love's keep.
Where your desires run true, run deep
as the endless sky, as the open sea,
under the guise of mystery,
born of ice and snow.

Dawn

Dawn dips her brush into her flaming breast,
paints bright streaks of fire across the morning sky.
Shades of peach and powder blue color the clouds,
tinge each frond and bloom with golden hues
that allow the heart to open its eyes,
the soul to see through the seamless sky,
in a stillness so beautiful, so true,
the stars themselves could cry.

Of Beauty's Love

The sunlight fell upon the rosebush,
made a sanguine pool of its blooms.
A robin came and dipped its breast
among the silken loveliness
of soft, sweet petals.
Then came a butterfly with golden wings
like two flakes of dancing sun,
landing lightly from bloom to bloom
then twirling as it rose above
and flew away to other heights.
Then came a fat bee to the bush,
a velvet tiger with mica wings,
busily burying its face in blooms,
driven to passionate foragings.
Then came a woman with a pair of shears.
I watched her as she gently clipped.
I saw blooms fall like bright, red tears.
I observed the way she lovingly slipped
the harvested blooms into a bag
whose braided handle lightly kissed
the slender wrist below her left hand.
When done, the woman strolled away,
her hips inclined to playful sway.
How beauty does seduce us all,
draws us in with her winsome call,
and we, like blossoms, helplessly fall, hopelessly in love.

Stones

I have always loved stones,
those chips off old mountain blocks,
born millennia ago from the slow
shuffle of glacial feet in their migration
through the ages.
Stones are the children of time and matter,
mineral babes tailored for the palm of the hand
or the secret corner of a pocket,
made to be skipped across ponds,
to be thrown,
to be scattered,
collector's pieces to be stored on shelves
or stacked in drawers,
fragments of this physical world neatly gathered.
A stone is so solid, so small,
a thing to hold onto, to rhythmically roll
between forefinger and thumb,
an object to toss in the air and watch it fall down,
a pebble to kick along a path and watch it glisten in the sun.
Stones endure, even when the fun and
promise of youth are gone.
Stones hold true to their nature, singing
their elemental song—
humming the secret of forever behind lips tightly sealed.
Stones are perfect treasures that make you feel the measure
of your worth in the holding.

Love Reverberates

I watched the young couple making love on screen.
He, deep in her young body, resolute and thrusting.
Her naked breasts before him, so vulnerable, so trusting,
waiting for his fingertips, for his hungry lips.
I almost gasped as I remembered the last time we made love,
what it was like to lose myself in sex, in love—
to come home to the goodness of the body.
To the point mind and flesh say, "I do."
Then to kiss the moment the world explodes,
dissolves into bliss— no control, just the ecstasy
of letting go, the overwhelming joy of coming
to know the boundless reverberations of love.

On Seeing the Painting of Pear and Peach

When I first looked at the painting, I
immediately fell under its spell.
Not that I am a connoisseur of Cubist
imagery, but something about
this painting's angularity was rich and
endearing and drew me to it,
instinctively.
The peach and pear made a handsome
duplet, delicately poised atop
a rectangle with a soft, yellow face and pale blue side.
The pear, two shades of blue, hoisted a stem erect as a penis.
The peach, two shades of salmon, offered
two green leaves spread wide
as willing legs in a dream of sex play suspended
above two bottles and a goblet.
The whole composition seemed to float
on a swatch of flying-carpet blue.
Background squares of pale green and yellow
collided like ice cubes in a glass.
Was it half full or half empty? I couldn't tell.
Having drunk so much of its symmetries,
this painting had inebriated me.
I only knew I wanted more until I could see
beyond the shapes, beyond the frame,
beyond the ideas in the artist's brain—all the
way down to the secret place where
the eye marries matter to form.

Two Squirrels Dancing

Two squirrels
slide up and down
the sides of a tree
like furry streams
of grey water.
They are searching
for food,
passing the morning hours
playfully.
The joy of living
coursing through
their squirrel veins.
The beauty of
their tree-trunk dance
is patterned in their
squirrel brains.
They are a miracle
of tiny paws
with dainty nails,
a mystery with
onyx eyes,
a masterpiece
with bottle-brush tails.
They are proof
that despite winter's paucity,
nature will triumph:

SEEING, BELIEVING, AND OTHER THINGS

life will prevail,
dancing merrily
through snow and gale
to the tune of spring
in their animal hearts.

Lessons Learned

I think I am happy—at sixty-four— retired two years,
a former professor, an ongoing poet.
The days finally belong to me; my time, my own.
There are no schedules to keep save those of my own making:
daily walks
daily writing
daily reading
daily praying
with my body, with my words.
Retirement, I have heard, can be challenging.
But I think that I was made for its freedoms.
I love the open-endedness of it—
the seeing and not seeing how I can live outside
the grind of workforce gears.
When I think back on my life now,
I spent too many years trying to create
the image of the person I thought the world
expected me to be,
rather than learning to love the person I was,
growing that image, setting him free.
In truth, that is the person I really am—
ever more so than the person framed on the wall,
composed of elegantly-scripted degrees.
I am ever the boy who watches the clouds
and talks to the trees,
who envies the birds and the graceful ease

SEEING, BELIEVING, AND OTHER THINGS

of their wings as they ride the wind.
I am the child of morning whose greatest sin
is loving this world enough to want to stay forever.
Going through it— getting to this point in life—
I never thought I'd survive,
never really believed I'd arrive
at a point when I would say, "Yes, I am blessed to be me!"
Yet here I am, happy as I stand
looking in the mirror at the *he* I am finally free to love.

Poem for My Age Spots

After my shower and shave, naked as I can be
in the electric glare of bathroom light,
I look at them in the steamed mirror.
Tiny dark islands, one on the left side of my forehead,
another in the fold at the edge of my left eye,
still others, in cluster, small archipelago
on my right temple, above the ridge of my cheek.
Their shores, uneven, uninviting, the jagged rocks of age,
slow ruination of this ship of face in
which I sailed through life—
that odyssey which seems more like a myth to me now
as I study these dark blossoms, fleurs du mal.
I am going moldy with age, the way the edges of the bread
turn blue in the plastic bag on top of the refrigerator.
I could cut them off, these spots on my face,
but the loaf of the body, like the loaf of bread
is already infected, already dead with spores.
Spoiler alert—everything falls to pieces in the end.
Neither laser nor scalpel, neither bread knife nor fingers
can remove the marks when Thanatos takes his crayons
to matter and begins to draw shapes and color them in.
I've imagined my death more than a thousand times.
Sometimes as grace? Sometimes as sin?
The question never answered.
The door, always locked, never lets me in.

Waking in the Dream

10:00 p.m.
I take Bella out for last business before bed.
She buries her face, her black leatherette sniffer,
in the dew-covered blades of dark grass,
nosing about for just the right spot to squat
and pee.
I stand there waiting, patiently,
a dark shadow self under cartwheeling stars
whose diamond-white dance makes me sigh
for all I cannot express, trying not to die
of the love I confess for this world, for my life in it.
For the way I've wept when I realize it must one day end.
But these are notions we go through—
notions we pretend are as real as the dark of night,
the burning campfires of stars who light the celestial plains,
letting us make believe we know where we are
in time, in space, that there is a place for us in God's heart.
Such actions, such urgencies as these:
like the meaning of life,
like the last pee for the night,
before turning off the light
before falling asleep,
before waking in the dream.

Beauty's Touch

Beneath the lily pads that form green islands
in the garden pond,
the koi move like shining dreams.
Sunset orange, moony white, hammered gold,
and calico,
they glide in silence,
cloistered nuns, fins rippling behind them
in soundless swish of silken habits.
If you look closely, you might see an air bubble
ascend,
a transparent pearl, rushing toward the surface,
an orb of breath taken and released,
expelled from blood red gills that open and close
in rhythmic ease,
as the koi swim, as the koi breathe in beauty
that touches your soul.

Expectation

Lately I've taken to looking at dying, at
the dead I find along the road—
The splattered possum, tiny furless fingers clutching death,
mouth frozen open in silent scream, the
bloodstain on the highway
the sharp teeth's moony gleam.
The doe lying on her side, mimicking full leap—
head thrown back, white arc of neck, legs
outstretched across the chasm
separating life and death.
The smell of the skunk that assaults the
nose even before the eye beholds
the smear of its body, decomposed, ground
into the gravel on the winding
shoulder of the road.
The shining cicada that looks like a brooch
with its cloisonne body and
mica thin wings,
the black barbs of its legs tucked
closely to its body as if to cling
to the memory of the buzz life once made.
All these visions are curiosities to me.
I am a neophyte to old age who needs to be
instructed in the proper way to approach death.
What procedure is correct?
What am I to expect beyond that final breath,
beyond the need to bleed.

When Dragonflies Dance

Two amber dragonflies with cellophane wings
do a helicopter dance among the last November blooms.
The leaves on the trees, the color of pennies,
shimmer in morning's light.
The earth is shifting gears,
slowing down to colder speeds—
foot on the break of the sun's healing heat.
Earth creates a wake of shriveling flowers, of dying leaves,
as she proceeds to other spheres, taking her warmth,
her maternal care with her as she goes.
The world behind her lies in wait for the comfort
of winter's snows to come and cover it,
tuck it neatly into bed, lullabye it softly to sleep
with night-wind songs it knows,
inviting spring dreams to dance in its head,
till it's time to rise—the joyful undead
whose life will begin again.

I Heard a Spider Singing

I was outside in the garden when I heard a spider singing,
a song so beautiful, I knew it must be true.
It sang in silken protein notes, in sweet spinneret refrains.
I listened carefully as its web-song grew, and in my heart
I secretly knew I was witnessing a miracle unfolding before
my eyes. As I watched the web change shape and size,
it seemed to spring from nothing but air. The song became
more intricate with each delicate score that appeared.
It was the song of a spider's soul, in blown glass strands,
a marriage of the spider's steady spinneret and busy hands
spun in a glistening web of sun. I stood and listened till
the spider's song was done. Then the spider sat paused
like a full note fixed, resting on the line of a staff,
a note, well sung, too high a pitch for human ears.
I remained in reverence like nature's true son,
attentively listening, straining to hear
the joyful ringing of web strands singing alleluias of light
through the air.

Ode to a Dead Cricket

It lay at the base line of the first step to our condominium--
one dead cricket.
A crisp copper creature on its back,
arms reaching skyward, legs outstretched
as if in mid-leap to the afterlife—
maybe a cricket heaven filled with joyful cricket song,
legs rubbing shrill alleluias.
This child of night's song,
this symbol of luck,
prized by eastern minds,
tended as guardian pets in tiny cages
with delicate bamboo bars, toothpick thin.
This conscience bearer who would chirp no more,
who would never leap again through the dew-spangled blades
of moon-bathed grass,
never squeeze through the crawl space between
the threshold and sweep of a closed door,
never hurl itself away from a hungry starling or
propel itself from the shadow of a sole approaching the floor.
This bronze husk of being on a concrete slab
was the handiwork of some artist's well-honed craft,
lying there waiting for someone to stop, for someone to ask:
Where does beauty go when it dies?

By a Thread

The spider was so elegant,
moving nimbly on ebony legs
across the tightrope her spinnerets
had flung from palm frond to window ledge.

She seemed a jewel gleaming with sun,
a shining pendant delicately hung
upon the wind's gently heaving breast.

I paused to watch her diminutive legs
caress the edges of silken strand
with the patience of a cloistered saint,
with the tenderness of a lover's hand.

She made her way, tiny acrobat,
traversing the world, a perfect fact
as stunning and simple as the act
of her indisputable being.

I stood in awe, amazed to see
this living wonder in front of me,
miracle of engineering and life set free
by a single wishful thread.

Things Ants Taught Me

I watch the ants, towering above them, the way Zeus
and his fellow gods and goddesses looked down upon
the earth from the cloud clothed heights of Olympus.
Today, the ants are toiling in tireless lines as they raise
the fine grain levees around sidewalk cracks,
in the center of each, a smooth mound, like a tiny ziggurat
strives heavenward in the infinitesimal orbs of its making.
I study the dark shine of the ants' copper bodies.
I know exoskeletons do not have pores,
that these industrious laborers are not living by the sweat
of their brows, but they are working as
if driven by a purpose divine.
What do they think of me standing over
them, observing their orderly lines—
a human cloud casting a dark shadow.
With one step, I could crush their intent,
sweep all their efforts away.
But the ants pay me no heed.
Maybe they do not fear fate, or the
gods, or the human debate to step
or not to step, to let them live or let them die.
I stand in awe of their drive to survive,
at their commitment to give all to their cause,
at their devotion to work without pause,
at their obedience to the laws nature has
written across their tiny ant hearts.
Mostly, I am stunned by their willingness to die trying.

Chasing the Sun

Lightning bugs in jars, blinking
luminescence, like God winking,
like stars gathered into jars called
galaxies, blinking luminescence
so we can see our way through space, through time.
Eternity folds over on itself again and
again until there is no clear
beginning, no clear end—just the
infinite present that lends itself
to dreams of future past.
Who knows what tomorrow will bring?
Who knows how long lightning bugs or stars in jars will last?
Unscrew the lids. Let them all fly away.
Their great migrations of light will
shape our desire to stay and
to pray until we finally get it right.
We, the children of the night, chasing the sun in our eyes.

A Spider's Life

Wiping the patio table clean,
I saw the little bundle of body and legs,
like the tiniest of tumbleweeds,
it danced across the tabletop
in the morning's gentle breeze—
the body of a baby spider, dead.
Small tangle of matter, rolling in the wind,
like a bit of dust,
like a grain of sand,
like a sin confessed and forgotten.
I paused in my task and decided
I would mark the occasion of one
begotten of web and beauty.
How when it lived, driven by
nature to survive, this spider
would give its all to its spinneret
to create a Fibonacci web—
precision and mathematical design,
the perfect place to lie in wait,
then crawl on nimble legs and wrap
its prey in silk, anticipating the meal.
How long had this tiny arachnid lived?
How long had its song of life been sung
before death took his fingertips and
rolled the spider into a ball of lifelessness
then flung it into a passing wind.

SEEING, BELIEVING, AND OTHER THINGS

I watched the spider's body blow away
and knew instantly in my heart that I
would write its eulogy, trying in my own
humble way to tell the world what the spider's
life meant, hoping the world would listen.

Love Requited

Today the ice plants smiled at me,
a wide, bright smile of purple blooms.
The sea grass whispered as I passed,
a pungent good day from the wind-swept dunes.
The sky was an accident of massive clouds
piled high above the sea.
The breaking sunrise poured sanguine streams
as the horizon began to bleed.
The gulls in homage or hunger screamed
their mournful cries.
I fell in love or maybe dreamed
I saw the face of God,
separating the mounds of clouds
with living light that seemed to shout
a luminous, "I love you, too!"

Gnat Fest

At first I think it's dust,
small burst of powdery debris
dispersed by an evening ocean breeze—
a dirty outside lamp that needs
a good cleaning.
On closer inspection, I see
a delirium of gnats
in love with light,
hurling their infinitesimal bodies
in wild abandon toward the bright,
belly of illumined bulb.
Dionysiac frenzy of flight,
they are willing to die, to be consumed
by the burning need—
spectral hunger for the glow that bleeds:
"Come to me. Come to me.
All you who hunger.
And you will be satisfied."

Considering My Grandsons

I take such pleasure in looking at my grandsons.
They are so wondrously wrought.
Works of nature at her very best,
  so perfectly formed: a young Adonis, a younger Apollo.
Their broad shoulders. Their muscled arms.
Their postures erect, so attuned, so alive to each move.
Watching them is truth I can believe.
I think of their sons, try to imagine who they will be—
  if I'll ever get the chance to see them.
But who could be that lucky to have the joy of watching
  truth unfold itself over time?
So I content myself with the blessings I have
  and cherish these wonders that are mine.
With pen and abundant heart,
I consign my feelings to these lines:
  a grandfather's gratitude and love,
  revealed in these humble rhymes.

BELIEVING

Pond Song

Today the pond has visitors, Canadian geese,
an even dozen gliding across its rippling surface,
the geese dip gracefully among the reeds
rigid with December's breath.
They are a prayer in motion,
feathered serenity at its best,
pure devotion,
creation passing the ultimate test
of God's love.

Love Is in the Proof

The fallen leaves scatter,
lift and swirl,
crisp revelations of
transitioning matter
captured and hurled
life after life.
I could chase them
like dreams I never dared,
murmur them
like essential prayers,
rustling "Mea Culpas"
whispered in God's ears.
The trees reveal themselves
willingly lay bare
their bark souls.
I can hear their resignation,
the stoicism of their self-control
that lets them happily acquiesce,
selflessly let go of all they were
to be who they are:
mirrors of divine majesty
demonstrating just how far
they'll go to prove their love.

This Moment of Truth

I worship You
each time I look up
at the moon
and fall in love
with its golden face
that sheds its light
like glowing grace
upon the night waters
of the bay.
I worship You
each time I try
to count the stars
those far-flung diamonds
of the night
that glitter and bejewel
the ebony sky.
I worship You
with each sound of
the night surf's breath,
each exhalation like
a little death in my soul.
I worship You
in the midnight clouds that roll
across the moon's bright cheek
and hide her loveliness
making me seek her beauty

P.C. Scheponik

in the corona of light that
leaks along the edges of clouds.
I worship You yesterday and tomorrow.
I worship You now,
in this moment of truth,
borrowed from the beauty I behold
in this world that surrounds me,
takes me heart and soul,
brings me to my knees
in a prayer that feels like love.

Stardust

I know you are there—
behind the stars.
I can hear You
beating in night's dark heart,
feel You in the stars' blue tears.
I am so small and the universe so large.
Yet You chase my smallness away
with Your stillness,
hold me in Your palms of light
where I kneel, one in wonder,
one in love—
knowing there is something of You in me—
something You have not forgotten,
teaching me to trust the fragile clay,
that dust of stars that lights my way
down the long, dark halls of Your love.

When Matter Sings

Matter sings and the song is beautiful. The song is true.
Oxygen and hydrogen's duet has made a symphony of seas.
Carbon's solo melodies have raised mountains, carved valleys,
have peopled the earth with flowers and trees,
have filled the waters with fishes, the air with birds, and
butterflies, and bees, the forests and fields with every kind
of man and beast that time's sacred womb could yield.
When matter sings, I can feel the notes in my cells keeping
time with the tempo, can hear the story matter tells in a song
as deep, as long as time.
When matter sings, I listen as if I'm
the only one in the audience,
as if matter's song was written and sung just for me.
When matter sings, I attend to its perfect melody—
each note sacred, each beat replete with the sound of eternity,
rich, vibrant, scored in the perfect key.
I give thanks each time that matter sings, thanks for the gifts
matter has given me—
a heart with the will to listen to the song.

Truth and Belief

The morning sky sings her blues,
reaching high notes of cream-colored clouds
and a sponge-print moon.
The goldfinches are already in the garden
their black feet clinging to
the spiny faces of coneflowers
as the finches industriously
forage for food with their ebony beaks.
The yellow swallowtail dances, at the peak
of his power, drunk on nectar and his hour
to find love.
The Queen Anne's Lace spreads the tablecloth
of her flowers across the field in preparation
for the feast, luring butterflies and bees
to celebrate, to drink, to eat their fill.
It seems the machinery of new day
cannot help but spill itself like life
in glowing currents of beauty bright,
glory of the morning light that fills the sky
with shine I can believe.

Walking Toward a Vision of Truth

This morning the sunrise followed me with her golden smile.
The scrub pines kept me company with
their armfuls of fecund cones.
A lone bald eagle with snow-capped head and wingspan wide
as a seraph's haunted the sky.
A throng of sparrows in a sycamore
tree performed like feathered
minstrels for me.
With lilting song and cheerful dance, they
filled my heart with light romance.
With little traffic on the road, my heart
reached in and touched my soul
so tenderly I was sure my mind would never be the same.
For I had seen the other side—the
perfect pleasure without the pain
of loneliness or loss that claims both joy and peace.
I buried both hands inside my pockets,
pressing down as deep
as they would go.
As if to hide from, as if to reach the
face of calm I've never known,
save in my yearnings, in my dreams
where I can gather ripened stars
from the galactic vines of eternity.
And my fingers don't burn. And the light is
sublime. And the darkness doesn't
frighten me anymore.

Love Story

The dune grass is nervous with light
in the late October wind.
The waves hurl themselves relentlessly
slapping the amber sand
with passionate intensity,
with glistening palms
of white-foam hands.
The sky, a rising sphere
of flawless blue glory
and cream-colored clouds,
has captured the sun,
and the gulls crowd
the air with beating wings
and cries that sound like
prayers of praise or songs
that sing of this world's beauty
cast in the truth of living things.
There are those moments
when time, itself,
touches the human mind,
a fingertip, delicately dipped
deep in the brain,
until it finds that place
where the sublime—
below the rivers of memory—
has traced its name,

like a hope for clarity
or a chance to reclaim
something possessed and mislaid.
These are the solar flares of the soul,
the sunspots of the heart,
generating pulses of remembered desire,
revealing the living art of God in each of us
that thrills and inspires for moments,
precious moments, that make us feel alive
in ways we've only dared in dreams.
Thus we find completion and a sense of purpose
and peace that reaches us from light years away,
like a promise of who we are, like a feeling that
a day can last forever, and forever is a love story
told by the stars.

The Echo of God Tears

The astrophysicists say that the light we
see from the stars is ancient—
that some glowing points may only be memories—
the stars who shed the light that fed those
flaming orbs are, in truth, long dead.
Their glimmerings are merely the echoes of
shine, bright wakes of their illumination.
That death, from light years away, could
be so full of absolute beauty,
so full of perfect truth, is a concept all consuming.
These diamond flickerings fill our minds with
wonder and our hearts with wishes.
Our destinies are writ in their white-ice kisses,
which wake us from the dark missives
of our longing, to be more than the span of a
handful of years, to be more than the centuries
built upon our fears, thronging ever
outward across the galaxies,
rolling timelessly as the tears down the
cheeks of a God who listens,
a God who hears our cries to be more,
so much more than we are.

The Devil in Us

Cry Antichrist. Cry Satan.
We see evil as some outward winged thing
breathing fire and seduction
encouraging sin and destruction
of body, of soul.
Cry lucifer. Cry demon.
Burn the witch. Bury the sodomite alive.
We know how to scape a goat,
create an evil to contain our black hearts.
Blind-folded children, spinning with our
paper-tail sins in our hands, we grope
for an ass to pin them on.
Cry temptation. Cry blame.
Threaten the sulfurous pit, the dance of endless flames.
Make a boogie-man devil for the game of life we play.
It's so nice to deflect, such a relief to digress,
to slip the noose of guilt, escape the stockade of regret
we carry within: the sorrow, the shame we beget—
deep, deep in the pit of hell nestled in the human heart,
dark thumbprint of hubris, that dangerous part,
when stirred to heat, lets us grow bat wings and horns,
arrow-tipped tails and serpent's teeth.
How we hide from the light.
How we whisper from forbidden-fruit trees,
"Bite, bite, bite your way to being God."

Fair Share

I am sitting here alone at the kitchen table.
She is already in bed asleep,
my wife, snoring lightly, busy in her dreams,
shoring up the seams of our life.
I am here with the open journal, its empty lines,
the pen in my hand, the need to write
something that matters more than the night,
more than the fears of age, of death, of the desire
to fight them all.
The need to protect myself from the knowledge
I might not matter to this world.
I think of the moon, marble smoothness of her pale cheek
coyly hiding behind satin clouds, then, coquettishly,
taking a peek to see if I am still staring.
Or the stars mindlessly burning, those engines
of eternity churning their fire into streams of light
that will feed my hunger long after they have died,
leaving me under the spell of believing, of wanting more.
I watch the words as they form on the lines, the letters as they
pour from the tip of the pen.
They are black, the color of blood before it hits the air,
the color of night when the soul throws open her doors,
when the heart strips bare, when all the universal laws
are called into question, when I extend my open palms
for my fair share of the answers.

Coming Storm

The thunderheads have sailed in,
docked at the horizon line—
battleships ready for action,
waiting to fire their electric flashes,
to light up the sky with thunderous passion.
The winds of war are rising—
stirring the waves to dissatisfaction,
whipping up their desire to break ranks,
to launch an attack on the defenseless sand,
to conquer the beach, to slaughter the dunes,
to raze the streets in an act of liquefaction
that could make the gods weep
for the memory of who they used to be.
Before the first two fish crawled out of the sea,
climbed up the helixed ladder,
named themselves Adam and Eve
and changed the ending of the story
to *unhappily ever after.*

Never Ending

Tell me there will be a day that never ends.
A sky that will always stay blue,
filled with cream-colored clouds
and a tissue paper moon
that looks like God's thumbprint.
Tell me there will be a sun
shining brightly on everyone,
on weeds and flowers in gardens fair.
Tell me this day will be filled with pristine
streams lined with daffodils.
Tell me that the scent of hyacinths will anoint
the air, that swallowtails will dance and soar
in synchronized pairs.
Tell me there will be only joy and nothing
to fear, and I will say, "Yes!" to forever.

Love Letters

Someone once asked me to talk about my poetry.
At the time, I couldn't describe, couldn't define
myself, my song, in any particular fashion that
this person sought. So I Simoned-and-Garfunkeled
a definition that sounded like silence. I'm sure my
interrogator found my response perverse— to be
so closed-mouthed about my verse, but, truthfully,
in my defense, I did not know how to answer in a
way that would make sense.
So now, years later, I have a response that I can
give— an answer to that someone or anyone who
wants to know what my poetry is.
My poems are love letters to God, to this earth,
to my wife, who is my lover, to our children,
whom she birthed, to my grandchildren, to
my great grandchildren, to my family, to my
friends, to the stars in the universe, to the
mountains, to the clouds, to the sea, to the waves,
to the gulls, to the shells, to the beach, to the birds
in the air, to the trees that reach for the sky, to the
rain, to the wind, to the sun who gives herself freely
that we might live another day, to the body, to the
soul, to the parts, to the whole, to the galaxy's eternal
roll. I sing of truth. All beauty I extol, with love—the
pure love of words.

Words

Today, the first words ran to me on stiff, black sandpiper legs,
spinning pinwheels across the wave-laced beach.
I followed them, listening to what they had to say,
attending to every flutter of wing and drill-bit beak
burrowing in the sand for something to eat.
Then the words grew puffed and grey as nesting gulls
huddled in the sand, among the shells.
Seasoned watchers of sea and land whose feathers stirred
with the wind's gusting swells, which compelled my mind
to thinking, my pen to linking these living things in a world
made of matter turned into words.
Chasing after the song, I heard crooning
under the thundering
surf, echoing upward toward the endless sky: words made of
foam and whelk and clam, words made of salt and sea glass
and sand, words made of matter by the mind's secret hands,
words that remind us of the God in the man.
Words, oh demiurgic words!

Love Child, That Time Before Morning

It is so good,
the morning,
before the sun
banishes the moon,
when the stars
burn diamond fire
across an indigo sky.
This is my favorite hour.
That in-between time.
The phase before
light and darkness kiss.
Not good. Not bad.
A span when there is
no choice to be made
no side to take
no need to be defined.
The space between
being asleep and
being awake.
Not quite night.
Not yet day.
Like the last fetal moment
down the dream-colored canal
into the bright light of life.
It is a gentle interval,
easy to go into,

a place I'd almost like to stay.
Here time or action
does not matter.
Here there is no need
to have a say.
The stars sing litanies
while the moon bathes
in blue solitude
that takes the fear,
the pain away.
Here there is no need
for mood.
Breath and vision will suffice
the sweet release from the
terrible vice of necessity.
Here judgement has no say
and the will in stuporous
surrender must lay its urges
aside.
Here Trust is groom.
Beauty is bride,
and Peace is their child of love.

In a Grain of Sand

Today the beach is naked,
save the lacy edges of waves
that drape the glistening thighs
of the outstretched sides of her legs
that lie for miles.
I am never so at peace, so happy to be
as I am walking the beach, just after sunrise.
I feel my feet sink into the sand
saturated with sea.
At times I almost feel one with my brother
and sister grains—
those star-born travelers whose ancient
claim to matter still lives in me.
I think I love them, their bucketfuls
of trillions, a number that makes me
unable to breathe when I try to imagine it,
like trying to look through the sky to see
God's face on the other side.
At moments such as these I try to visualize
what it will be like once I'm cremated and
pulverized—after this life of the body is done,
and I, transformed, once again become
an infinitesimal, granular one.
After they have spread my ashes upon the waves,
and I am free, finally free.
How I will rush home to the countless faces

SEEING, BELIEVING, AND OTHER THINGS

that wait for me on the beach,
take my place among them in tight cellular unity
that sings earth's song eternally through
salt-grain lips,
that praises the dance of galaxies that
offer the chance to be and be again—
infinity swimming in a grain of sand,
singing in everlasting refrain:
I am ... I am... I am.

Amber and Rust

Tell me your secret,
Oh mist-bathed Moon,
haloed in rings of amber and rust.
Tell me a tale
of lovers doomed,
of lives consumed by passion and lust.
Tell me how men
have followed you,
driven mad by your luminous light.
Tell me how you've
lured them to love
with wiles and mystery
their wills could not fight.
Tell me how Time
has given you sway
over matter and mind
and the games Fate plays
with the lives and loves
and the endless graves
that form the finale
on this human stage
in the shades of lost souls
in the hearts that break
in your wreaths of amber and rust.

True Story

If not a journey, what is this life
but a passage of years,
a collection of sighs,
of laughter we use to hide our fears,
of tears we cry when we cannot bear
the weight of the hearts we break
to protect our own,
of the beds we make and unmake
till our bodies find a soul they can sleep with.
It's really about what we take,
more than about what we give,
telling ourselves that the stars write
their stories across the sky for our paltry sakes,
or that the sun will rise, and the moon make
itself full to light our errant way.
If life is not a purposed quest, then who's to say
there is a reason for our being,
that we're not just happenstance of a dance of proteins
and amino acids freeing the genie molecules and gasses
from lamps of would-be minds,
or that maybe reality is just a ball of strings that unwinds
randomly over time, telling a tale neither meaningless nor
sublime to ears that will never hear the truth in the story,
no matter how they try.

Stepping into Love Time

Today the sky was blue divinity
interrupted by a staccato of Monet clouds.
Each a hosanna, a prayer made of molecules of love
singing "Gloria" in shifting scales.
My eyes fell back in the ecstasy of the moment
when beauty leaned in and embraced truth.
I was their shared kiss.
The words spilled from my lips,
like a bell rung for the glory of the sun
poured down upon the sea.
The white diamond waves rushing,
driven by their need to reach the beach,
plant their hungry kiss while there was still time.
Before the sun would set and the pale moon rise
to begin her evening journey,
climbing the starry ladder of night's sky.
Oh absolute! Oh blessedness!
The *I* that reached inside the *Am*
and delivered a universe
that would unfold like a flower
to proclaim an island of love
in Time's eternal hour,
to give me one moment
in the glory, in the power that was mine.

When Stars Fall

I know that stars fall from heaven—have fallen—
Lucifer was one, maybe the brightest of them all.
Yet You let him go—
gave him his wings, his beauty, his angelic will
whose choices couldn't be changed.
There was no apple, no serpent to seduce—
just a once-and-future tree with a God-man hanging
between Heaven and earth—a yin to a yang.
What was it that made this Morning Star, this Bearer of Light
decide to raise his will like a flaming sword, to refuse You
who gave him all but what he needed—the desire to obey,
to stay in Your mansion made of many stars, loving you
with each beat of his wings.
Did it break Your Father-heart when he turned his back
to Your face, refused to kneel, refused to sing
"Gloria in Excelsis Deo" above that cave in Bethlehem
where the wonderling lay swaddled in lamb's wool,
in flesh and bone, homeless, wingless, helpless in the cold
night of rebellion's hold on Your lost angel-son whose hands
would never fold in supplication?
Did You weep for the shadow Your fallen
son cast over all creation?
Or did you walk silently behind him like one at a distance,
stepping into his darkness, opening Your starfire mouth,
sighing constellations whose brightness,
whose beauty could never

P.C. Scheponik

fill the dark corner of Your heart left
void when Lucifer closed his
great wings and fell from the empyrean,
never to sing your love again
in time, in space, heart hardened against
the race that took his Father,
his birth right away, like a thief in the deep, dark night.

Wordburst

Some say poetry is a religion,
a search for truth made of words
that cut a covenant of heart,
make it bleed.
Some say poetry is an art,
the ability to melt words down
to our basic needs,
fashion golden claves we can dance before
polishing their hooves with our lips and hair
till we can see our reflections in our idols' feet,
dare to pretend we have the power to be
more than the sounds of our cries in the dark.
Our words, the arks that hold all we have
of hope, of fear, of dreams.
Our words that shadow our every move
with demon and angel wings.
Our words that leave us the way the body leaves the soul
that rise in a chorus and sing in judgment
against hands that stole the fire.
These letters that when rubbed together
ignite in a burst of words.

Only the Lost Can See

The leaves have all fallen.
Like years, they lie in heaps,
laundry piles,
waiting to be cleaned,
their dirty secrets bleached
away.
The bare branches of the trees exposed,
naked as the truth fear had hoped
to conceal forever.
The past is life's skeleton—
bones too clever not to be rattled,
snake coiled, ready for battle,
to strike chords of sorrow
that bite into the heart
until yesterday bleeds into tomorrow,
and memory seems like a dream of today.
There is no escape from this game of charades
the living play.
Even after death we do our best
to pretend we know the way out of the forest,
but the naked trees reach out and grab us,
snag and tease us with their sharp edges and
twisted roots that trip and strip till we see the truth,
bleeding profusely before our eyes, giving us pause,
a chance to realize how fallen, how lost we really are.

Star Love

I looked up and saw the clouds and said,
"I am in love" with glory,
with playfulness of changing shape,
with ecstasy of flying.
I looked up and saw the sky and said,
"I am in love" with the great blue bowl
of emptiness that hides the night,
that arcs as deep and endless as the sea,
that invites me in to swim toward infinity.
I looked up and saw the sun and said,
"I am in love" with fire,
with the raging flames
I see each time I close my eyes,
burning blue and gold streaks across my mind,
a thousand dark spots in swirling ascent,
like starlings in late afternoon light.
I looked up and saw the stars and said,
"I am in love" with light
that lives and light that is dead,
light that dwells in me, after eons, again,
as if God took me by the hand and said,
"Arise and come forth from the tomb of night,
to love the fires burning bright in My heart,
and to know they burn for you."

The Coming God Hour

I can feel my soul
outgrowing this body.
like a cicada ready to leave its husk.
My soul sings a song
of needing to be freed.
Like a bird beating its caged wings
against the bars—
the need to fly outweighs
the need to feed or breed.
I love these hands that let me hold,
these ears that let me hear,
these eyes that let me see,
this nose that lets me breathe the air,
this flesh that lets me be.
But now there is a voice drawing near—
calling…calling me.
It sings of sunspots and nebulae,
of stars whose lumens are
too far away to see,
of dark matter alcoves and wormhole halls
of dimensional blends and secret bends
of gravity.
I can feel the atoms dancing in me,
their dervish swirls like spinning suns.
I can sense the tension of their power
building toward the supernova hour

SEEING, BELIEVING, AND OTHER THINGS

when they all explode
when I become one with time and space,
with matter that runs like quantum grace,
dripping from the fingers of God.

My Youngest Brother Calls Me

Tonight my youngest brother calls me
to tell me how his disease has progressed—
the weakness moving throughout his body—
anaconda slow, constrictor hold.
This time the left hip no longer pivots.
He describes how he cannot swing the hip,
bend the knee to put on his pants.
How he needs an arm-long clip
to grab the waist, guide the pants up each leg—
At fifty-three he is older than me,
twelve years his senior.
I tell him how sorry I am, how unfair this is!
I promise I will pray for him.
I don't tell him how I don't understand
how God would let him have this disease,
anymore than I understand how God let him suffer
the hatred, the beatings, the mockeries he endured
because he was born a boy who would grow up
to be a man who would love a man.
I don't tell him how I think life is cruel
and fate sadistic, and the thought that he
will one day be locked in a body heavy as cement,
one that will drag him down under the water,
drown him in his own saliva.
These thoughts are too ugly to have—
maybe too ugly to write.

SEEING, BELIEVING, AND OTHER THINGS

But though they lack even an iota of beauty,
they are heavy with truth—dead weight heavy,
heart-crushing heavy, soul smothering heavy.
So I tell him I am sorry.
I tell him to keep me posted, as if talking were a cure.
I tell him I love him before I say goodbye and hang up.
These words alone are good, are pure.
These words alone are the only things I am sure of
in this world of chance and odds stacked against us.
Even the strongest believer,
Even the greatest dreamer
walks away with only what this world is willing to give.

Because

It was one of those nights I just couldn't sleep,
having *prayed the Lord my soul to keep*.
I just couldn't let go of consciousness.
So I got out of bed— rose like Lazarus
from the dead of night and went outside
to challenge the stars.
Their bright intensities were burning
like the *Whys* in my mind.
And I swear the night sky seemed like eternity.
And the moon was too busy being poetry
to notice me or to answer my longing.
But the crickets in Gregorian unity
with ebony-legged impunity
chanted this simple refrain:
Because…

Maybe

Maybe it was an indigo bunting I saw land
on the weeping willow branch—
bright blue jewel singing in a shower of chartreuse leaves.
I felt my heart sprout wings and rise
with each note of beauty's song.
I sensed the world's living glory
in every root, branch, and leaf—
how each longed for the sun's kiss,
the warmth of golden lips
loving them to life.
My soul seemed to blend
with the sky,
to reach out and over as if
to hug the whole of this world—
till the bunting's song and I were
one joy spoken, one truth sung,
for a moment I thought would
never end.
Maybe there was no bird at all,
no willow tree or song,
no heart with wings or
sky made of soul.
Maybe there was just a man
in love with this world and no
way to hold onto this love except
with the hands of these words.

No Match for the Heart on Fire

What is more beautiful than being loved
and having loved in return?
I'm telling you,
the sun for all his sacred light
is no match for the heart on fire with love.
The moon for all her silver glow
can never share, will never know
the passion, the pleasure of making love.
The stars whose glory spangles the night
will never kiss another's lips.
The mountain peaks that pierce the clouds
can never brush another's brow
with tender lover's fingertips.
The ocean with his mighty waves
can traverse this wandering earth,
but will never have the chance to say,
"I love you," with its surf.
The wind for all her majesty
rushing here, then there
will always roam this world alone
on journeys never shared.
The plains for all their rolling wonder
have no lover to lie under.
The grandeur of their outstretched forms
remain a passion never borne.

SEEING, BELIEVING, AND OTHER THINGS

For all the beauty that they hold,
earth and cosmos can never know
the joy of giving and receiving
love that has no bounds.

Tides of Grace

There is a silence, a sacred space one finds at the beach,
where each may seek a favorite place
in the healing heart of the sea.
Oceana, you molded us over an eternity of time, of space.
Your saltwater fingers braided us in the roar
of your love, in the tides of your grace.
You made us one with the infinite space
between each grain of sand.
You are the power of creation. Our hearts are in your hands.
You fill our souls with your white-capped
dreams, instilling in us a love sea deep.
Here is a total more than the sum of its parts.
Oceana, in the bounty of your wave-worn
heart, you bathe us in your serenity.
In the cradle of your rocking, we learn
to love as we learn to be.

White Anglers

In the depths of the sea,
where the sun's bright fingers
never reach
those secret places
dark as God's hidden heart,
the white anglers dwell.
Luminescent as angels,
sharp-toothed as the crags of hell.
They are fruitful.
They multiply.
The two shall be as one.
The male eats of her flesh,
latching on,
until their cells mingle
and they become
one body and one blood.
A light in the darkness
of inner space,
the galaxy of her eggs
brought to life by the grace
of his sperms' flood
in the triumph of darkness
over light.
The word is spoken:
"Let there be life!"
And the sea becomes
token of God's delight,
and the waves whisper: "It is good."

Goodwill News

Today I saw her,
in the Goodwill Store
in Punta Gorda, Florida—
Mary, the Mother of God
in a bowl.
Queen of Heaven in laminate,
resting among jeweled buckles and barrettes.
I wondered how
it could come to this—
articles of faith,
piled in a place—
the leftovers of life.
Mother of Wisdom,
Mother of Grace,
for sale with other
loose odds and ends.
The line between real
and make pretend
blurred for one nascent moment.
What is sacred
and what profane?
What is mad
and what is sane?
In this place
where joy and pain
can be bought for less than a dollar.

Morning Prayer

The first shafts of sunlight
break into smile,
gild the edges of mountainous clouds,
pour golden lumens upon the waves,
mark the birth of another day.
I am ocean born,
in love with sky and sea,
drawn along, drifting on
this rolling white-capped majesty.
There is a beauty born,
a truth in me.
I am being
carried in matter's unerring embrace.
I am become a thing worth saving,
an expression of indelible grace.
There is nothing more to do
than feel,
nothing more to say.
So real, this moment,
so perfect, this day.
All that remains is worship and this poem,
praying from this page.

Night Song

February's wind howls
like an arctic wolf.
The full moon seems
carved in ice—
cold blue light
staring from an onyx sky
amid the diamond tears of stars.
Those ever-watchful eyes of night
know who we are,
who we pretend to be,
living out our little lives
threading our oh-so-humble lines
through the evolving tapestry of time.
We hope for something more than death:
a body that is more than bread,
blood that is more than wine.
How we stand wooled against the cold.
How we cry in sorrow to save our souls.
How we try with futile hands to hold
the image of who we are.
Ultimately, truth be told,
we are made of wounds
and made of scars,
and know not what we do.

The Flowers Give

The flowers joyfully give
their souls up to the sun—
offering tabernacle petals
as beds for bees and butterflies,
and throats as chalices for nectared light,
sweetened with the gift of life,
their pollen prayers cast to the air
by countless wings and breath of winds
that circle earth in endless quest
to bring to life the strongest and the best
this world has to offer.

The Imprint

On such a beautiful day as this,
I could drink the sun,
long, golden draughts of it,
fill my soul with its warmth,
my heart with its life.
I was born of stardust and God spittle,
a paste to make a love-child of light,
one scared of the dark,
one in love with the shine
of sun on waves,
diamond teardrops that could raise
the dead from their deepest graves.
I am bathed
in the goodness of God,
my heart, engraved
with His fingerprints of light.

The Longing

This morning the half-moon hung in the sky
like a piece of paper, a cubist smile cut into
a perfect arc, standing on end.
The sky, pale blue iris of a lovestruck God,
looked down with the love of a long-lost friend.
I followed the flight of a solitary gull
whose sharp-winged trajectory carried me
to a place I longed to go—wild and free,
beating the feathered extremities of my soul
against the doorway to eternity, to the secret,
to the mystery that lies behind the love of the
sky's blue eyes.
I wanted to give homage to the Maters and Paters
of the stars. I wanted to find my lineage in the
galaxies that lie inside the God in me, the One
who keeps me sliced thin as this paper-moon smile.
I wanted more than this day could give with its glory
of sun, with its grandeur of sky, more than this
ecstasy of longing to fly home to the full heart
of love that cries ,"Wholly,! Wholly! Wholly!"

An Easter Morn of Sorts

The sea and sky formed an Easter
Sunday glory of light, of calm.
The waves, silken hillocks of lumens,
poured themselves like grace upon the shore.
I thought, for a moment, Christ might come walking,
robed in white purer than clouds—
wounds, blood bright and shining fresh as new love.
I imagined He might walk to me, kneeling on the beach,
touch my forehead with His fingertip and reach
that part of me, the way the Father touched Adam to life
in Michelangelo's Sistine dream of faith,
the way Thomas, the doubter, pressed
his deep probing finger of need to believe
in something greater than his own humanness,
greater than the beauty of this sea, this sky.
This need we have to be— even after the tide recedes,
leaving behind all the broken pieces of this life we find
along the edges of death and loneliness.
This losing that is everything we guessed
it would be in the end—
the need for salvation, for making pretend
we matter enough not to die.

Things Made

The sky is moody this morning. Maybe he's
sad because he had to give up the stars
for another performance of sun, that bright egoist
of light. Maybe the sky's grey brooding
is the result of what we have done to the earth
and the sea, our twin mothers who, together,
knitted this helixed destiny of terrestrial life, who
molded our eyes to behold celestial heights,
who fashioned our minds for dreams of flight. Maybe
the sky's grim visage is born of boredom
and nothing more—the need to fold up his great
grey tent and move on to other galaxies, other
worlds—his dark desires piled into mountains of
nimbus clouds. Maybe the sky is simply tired
of not being allowed to let go of our blue water
earth—not being able to make a sail of his great
self, to catch a cosmic breeze and hoist away on
an odyssey made of something more than
stories of earthbound men. Maybe the sky dreams
of being God—all that lightning and wind has
given him delusions of grandeur, made him believe
he is more than molecules of dust and gas.
Maybe those sullen shades the sky wears this
morning, that tumult of layered blends,
that troubled expression on the sky's face, is just
the look of realization, the full grasp of his fall
from grace, the knowledge that he is but
a thing made and nothing more.

Psalm

Give me the stars at night.
Let me rise with the moon,
fall with the trailing light
of meteors burning bright.
Let me lie with dandelions
whose constellations bless the sight
of all who gaze upon them.
Let me swim the mountain stream,
beat with the heart in the sunfish's side
like a golden dream—
so beautiful, so true, so alive
I could believe in forever.

Losing Myself

I could lose myself in the clouds,
soft white musings of God's mind.
I could stretch myself out
on the blanket of blue sky,
let the sun cover me with golden kisses.
I could be one with the wind's cool majesty—
ruler of gulls' wings, turner of leaves.
I could pour myself like sand on the beach,
each glistening grain of me bleached
by the sun, swallowing the sea with
each wave that runs over me,
moved by the sudden rush of love.

Oceanus Hymn

You call, and I come running to your waves, rushing like love.
You are still beautiful, though I am not.
You are still full of mystery, though I am not.
You are boundless energy, though I am not.
You are endless possibility, though I am not.
I love your grey waves, their milk-white foam.
I love the thunder of your heart.
I ache with the yearning of your salt-rush groan—
reaching, always reaching for the shore to make your own.
The beach lies in waiting, each grain
anticipating the taste of your salt lips.
You call me, and I come, bringing all my love,
holding my errant wish in my hands—
my unfinished heart, my perfect gift of longing.

The Making

Each step I take is another word of praise—
the body, saying a prayer of motion,
giving glory for the muscle,
giving worship for the bone,
giving adoration for the blood
that makes a home of this living tabernacle
of heart-beating love,
of blessed breath that pours forth from lungs,
of eyes that gather the morning's light,
of ears that sing the songs of sound,
of tongue that dwells within the mouth
to taste this milk-and-honey world,
of flesh that feels both flowers and rain,
the warmth of a palm, the curve of a face,
the deep desires of love's embrace.
Oh, the power! Oh, the glory!
that runs through my legs,
carrying me home to that sacred place,
to the stardust and God-spittle used to make me
who I am.

OTHER THINGS

The Sorrow and the Shame

He says he wants to go home to die.
He doesn't want to spend the last moments
of his life in the hospital—take his leave from
this world in a rented bed, attended by those
paid to take care of the almost dead—
making the rounds of the bodies hanging on—
his candle melted down, his life still clinging
to the curled crescent of charred wick,
the tiny ember on the very tip like the spark
of God that no longer fits his failing body.
The cancer has conquered, and his body
has quit fighting. The systems are closing down
one after the other, and there's no reigniting
the power to heal or the will to live.
There's just his request, that they listen,
that they give him what he asks for—
to let him go home, to let him die
in the bed he calls his own.

What of Forever

I will not leave my life unwritten,
though I will go into that night untyped.
My words lying on pages the color of moon
reflecting the light of sun my eyes no longer see.
My words, drying on these lines, on these pages
growing brittle and brown around the tips,
like bodies of fallen leaves, curled and crisp—
those left along the edges of walks and roads
and the root-gnarled bases of trees.
Who will love the piles poised on the promise
of being read, of reaching out and speaking
after I am long dead?
Such a Lazarus tease that plays in my head…
that plays in my head.
I have sanctified the pen.
I have made a paper bed for my heart to
lie down upon, for my mind to pretend
that my soul might live forever.

There Comes a Point

There comes a point when the best thing
we can do for our children is die.
Before the mindlessness and madness
pry self from body, turn consciousness to dust,
proving there is a purgatory and therefore must
be a hell, where the body becomes a fragile shell
crushing hopes and breaking hearts—
a horror show of creeping parts that break and
bleed and ooze.
But most of all to show us how little we are and
how much we have to lose.
Such great capacity to wound and leave nothing
behind but the scar to serve as a reminder we are
never far from suffering.
How an hour becomes an eternity in time,
and the only hope for escape we can find
is through death's merciful door.

Learning to Read at 63

Now that I am retired, my life is like the last
chapter of a book I don't want to end.
So, I am reading it slowly—line by line, one
word at a time, savoring each inference
and essence that I find as I read, as I breathe the
words in and out like air. Each moment
willingly surrenders itself like a sacrificial lamb
on the altar of time, neck pulled back,
waiting for the blade, the push, the pull, the rush
of blood that finds the meaning behind
the scarlet curtain, which hides the nowhere
between who I am and who I was meant to be.
If only I had been willing, if only I had been able
to read between the lines, I might have
seen the real story being told.

Of Promises and Keeping

The moon is a smooth ivory disk pressed
against night's ebony cheek,
a silent, self-contained, wandering waif
who monthly seeks a place to stay,
to be whole, to feel safe. In her travels, the
moon regularly keeps her promised
dates with tides and time, and she never
breaks her vows to follow night or
dutifully to shine her gracious light upon the
earth once sun has fled in the hope
to birth another day. Then the moon is
celestial queen reigning over the eternal
gleam of countless starry eyes who seem to
stare in perpetuation at the infinite
machinations of time and space. And we
of flesh, and we of blood cast up our
eyes in awe to face our deepest, darkest fear:
We are all alone in the pitch of night, and
the moon and the stars don't really
care how lonely or how frightened we are.

Last Chapter

In this last chapter of my life,
let me do much more
than see and write.
Let me spread my wings
and graze the clouds with gulls.
Let me dance with foam
upon the waves' sleek swells.
Let me sunbathe in the sand
with the scallop and whelk shells.
Let me waver in the wind
with grassy dunes.
Let me sing nature's glory
with the ebony loons.
Let me follow the sleepy sun
to her crimson bed.
Let me shine like a harvest moon
when I am dead.

Things of This World

The sky, battleship grey.
The sea, a misty milk plain,
silent and serene against
the navy-blue thread
of horizon that seems
too thin to hold the sky and sea
together.
A white-breasted gull soars by,
shatters the calm
with the piercing need
of its cry—
hunger for the sea,
hunger for the sky,
hunger for the things
of this world.

Time's Promise

Time makes a solemn promise
to us all:
to bring us to this world,
let us walk a while,
to show us both of beauty
and of truth,
the ecstasies of pleasure,
the agonies of pain,
to let us fall in love
with life's very breath,
then with neither
rhyme nor reason,
to introduce us to our deaths.

The Understanding

Though I live to write these words on these lines,
they cannot give me life.
They are just a way of holding on to an idea of who
I am.
How I number myself among the multitude of leaves
on the trees, or stars in the sky, or waves in the sea.
Who am I?
Who am I?
How can I be of any significance amidst all I see
of beauty, of beauty's truth surrounding me
in this world.

For the Woman Crying at Kohl's

She was sitting on the bench in front
of Kohl's department store,
her blonde hair pulled back into a
pony tail, the kind my sisters
used to wear when they were girls.
She was wiping her eyes and eating
what looked like a sandwich
of some kind, picking up the small
pieces that fell on her blouse,
the color of peaches.
She was crying as she reached into her pocket, took a tissue,
and dabbed her eyes.
I wanted to go over and tell her I was
sorry. I wanted to give her
a hug and tell her it would be all
right. But she was huddled in
the shadow that was hugging the wall,
and I felt a barrier—invisible—
yet it still gave me pause.
I didn't know her or the cause of her
grief at all, and I had no right
to assume I could make a move to
comfort her, to stop her tears,
to prove better days were, in fact, coming.
So I walked away, the sense of her grief
pressing down upon me.

SEEING, BELIEVING, AND OTHER THINGS

How could it be—this thing called
empathy—this impulse to feel
another's misery, yet not able to heal
it, to take it away, to only be
permitted to watch and see the ordeal, to
sigh for her, even cry for
her, maybe even pray for her from afar.
So I wrote these words for, you, the
woman crying at Kohl's on a
Tuesday morning. Though I could not
close your wound, at least
I can honor its scar.

The Need

I see the runners every morning jogging
faithfully down Coastal Highway:
women with their sports bras and jaunty
pony tails wagging side to side
and men in their muscle tees or shirtless,
wearing Armor-all shorts.
All of them in their Nikes "just doing
it" against the concrete walk,
the sweat glistening off their bodies bathed
in sun and wind from the run.
And then there are the bikers sporting
headgear and spandex, pumping
their grueling spin of wheels— vulcanized
rubber meeting the road.
I, too, am one of them, but not one who
runs, not one who rides along
Coastal Highway making strides in strength and confidence.
I am one who opens the journal; the
blank pages spread like wings.
I am one who flies across the lines letting
the tip of my pen skim the
waves of thought the way the gulls and
ospreys search for the streaks
of tails, the glint of fins of those silver-
bellied dreams that swim just
under the surface, the way the ideas

SEEING, BELIEVING, AND OTHER THINGS

glide beneath the edges of
consciousness to be plucked from
possibility that is suddenly turned
real—a metaphor, a simile.
I'm telling you, I can make a meal of a
poem, the hunger in me so strong.
I can feel its need to break out and run
free with all the other fitness buffs
I see every morning chasing destiny that stretches
before them like Coastal Highway.

Book of Life

These days, I am holding the book of my life in my hands,
the last thin chapter between my thumb and forefinger.
I'm so careful when reading the lines—no skimming—
no skipping to the end, which is so much closer than I
ever thought. I am reading slowly now, living each word fully,
enjoying the crunch of consonants, the burst of flavors from
the vowels. I am devouring my life—savoring each second.
I am like the starling with my head buried in summer grass,
foraging for seed to feed my soul, to
fill me with joy, to let me
hold onto every moment of every
day. I am like the young boy
at the edge of the lake, looking for the sudden silver flash of
minnows—scooping with my heart,
dipping it deeply in, like a
net so as not to let one small moment
wriggle its tail and swim
away. I am like an old playwright,
editing the folio of my final
play, the one I don't want to end, the
one where the world's the
stage, and the pace is anything but
petty, and the only sound of
fury is the beating of my own heart.

The Fear

I wake at 3:45, the stars still grazing in the sky.
Dawn, bright shepherdess, has not yet
called them back to darker folds,
places hidden in deep space
where the stars grow old and die.
I hold the pillow closer,
press my face into its feathered mold
and stare into what's left of night—
what's left of life, of hope this story
can be told without a veil of tears.
I believe in endings.
I know they play their necessary parts—
but it's the fear of denouement
with its conquered spirit and broken heart
that haunts me, makes me want to hold on,
makes me watch the backs of fading stars
even as they wander away.

In Comparison

I watch the young father open the
passenger-side door of his Volvo
and commence the task of fastening
his toddler into the child seat.
Straps criss-crossing his son's chest like
a "cross my heart and promise
you will not die."
Such care this young father takes today, such love for his son.
But does he love his boy any more than I loved mine?
I who sat my son in the front seat with me—
used my arm as seatbelt at sudden stops
to keep him injury free—
to keep him whole, to make sure that
he would live and grow up
to one day have a son of his own.
What did we know back then, when a
hamburger cost fifteen cents,
and we shopped at Woolworth's and
the Five and Ten cent store.
What did we know of air bags and car
seats to keep our kids safe?
We knew to remove the doors of old refrigerators.
We knew to take the dry cleaners
plastic bags, "to tear them up,
to tie them in knots, to throw them away."
We knew not to let our children swim in neighborhood pools

SEEING, BELIEVING, AND OTHER THINGS

after the rain so they wouldn't catch polio and have to live
in an iron lung or wear braces on underdeveloped legs.
We knew what we knew, but it wasn't enough to keep
our children safe from danger, safe from harm.
Death has a way of letting himself in,
no matter how deeply we love, no matter how hard we try.
The end is written before we even begin.
And after we learn to pray, we learn to cry.

Something Important

I worry about the absence of making love in my life,
the empty space in my soul waiting, needing to be filled,
like the empty space between your legs, behind your lips
closed in a sideways frown—
as if something is missing, something important.
Like losing touch with ourselves, with this world as physical
as mountain rock and marsh mud, tree bark and pansy petals.
I hear the robins singing spring.
I watch their red-breast battling, staking territorial claims.
I can feel the world moving on, and I know there is a name
for what I feel—
left behind.
Life's reign for me, for us, is turning the
corner, path of setting suns.
Night can't be far behind, and we are the ones left in the dark,
reaching out, taking hold of each other to ward off the fear,
to defeat the cold, waiting for the promise of stars.

Eleventh Grade English (For Peter Doyle)

He told me I had to choose—be a preacher
or a poet—I couldn't be both.
So many years later his words wake up, a
sleeping dog at the back door
of my mind, stretching, arching its back,
then scratching to get out, or in—
barking if I don't answer right away,
growling if I say, "Sit!" "Stay!"
Baring its teeth that gleam in the half-light of memory,
bright and sharp as biting truth that
would still make me bleed after
all these years.
He, long in the sleeping earth, me, an
old man more yawn than waking.
Still, that rebel student in me, the one
more interested in breaking
the rules than obeying, part preacher, part
poet, who loves the tasting
and the making of poems that try to do both.

Oh Night, My Friend

Again, I sit with you,
oh night, my guardian, my friend.
Your starry eyes are filled
with love that knows no end.
How they dance and burn, your eyes,
with a look that does not pretend.
Alone in this chair, by this lamp,
with these lines, on this page,
with this pen in my hand,
I chronicle the time we share,
trying to understand
how a being as ancient as yourself
could befriend a man such as me,
could care that I am,
would take the time out of eternity
to spare my heart its loneliness,
to quell its fear, to grant it ease,
to kiss my closed eyes with your dark lips
and with the solace of your stars,
to garland all my dreams.

My Place in the Family of Things

I want to know my place in what Mary Oliver calls
"the family of things."
I would like it to be somewhere between
the roll of ocean waves and the soar of seagull wings.
If it can't be there, then let my place be
between the falling drops of rain that make the pond
sing hymns in rings that grow in elegant refrains.
If my place can't be there, let it be among the joyful
notes that spring from the sparrows' throats
on summer mornings.
If my place can't be there, let me live buried in the
sunny florets of a dandelion's face.
If not there, let me race on sandpiper legs
along the surf's edge of foaming white lace.
If my place isn't there, let me find my home
among white pine needles and their resinous cones.
And if not there, let me dance with the stars
bejeweling the night sky between Venus and Mars.
Let love give me shelter.
Let love keep me far from the war in my heart.
Let love heal all my battle scars.
Let love teach me the art of forgiving.

The Art of the Poem

Sometimes, when I try to make a poem
longer than it wants to be,
the words and images take up arms against me—
rebel at my alignments,
revolt at my constraints,
murder my careful strategies,
mangle my deepest aims.
Sometimes the art of the poem has little to do with pleasure
and more to do with the pain
that comes from trying to measure beauty,
to unearth the treasured truth.
Sometimes when I try to make a poem
do what I want it to do,
the poem, like a spiteful child sits down,
legs crossed, arms folded and refuses to move.
And no matter what I say, how I finagle, how I brood,
the poem just won't give me my way.

No Surprise to the Stars

Auschwitz has always lived in the human heart,
its blood flames burning.
Tongues of hungry hatred devouring all in us
that would be, could be good.
The stars stare down in pitiless glare,
unmoved, unsurprised by how we dare and drive
ourselves to contrive more efficient ways to kill,
to die through the devices of our minds,
malignant with the lies we tell ourselves
about "the other" we would gladly crucify
on an iron cross with a barbed wire crown
of thorns.
In how many ways, how many times must God die
before we can live, can see the truth before our eyes
that "the other" is our chance to give ourselves back
to who we are, who we have always been—
a species born to look up, to touch the stars
with our longing, to find an end
to the emptiness that fills our darkest parts
that pretend to be all, that tend to take all
like false friends, giving nothing in return
but the feeling of being burned by the flames
that were meant to warm, to protect us from
the black-ice night of fear.
There is a song in the universe we cannot hear
for the blood-rush thrumming in our ears.

Its notes are made of distant light,
breaking into day,
interrupting the dark night of our souls when we listen,
creating stars on our lashes that glisten
like sunshine and smiles,
that make this life we live worthwhile,
that soothe the savage, human guile
prowling our collective hearts.

And what of Poetry

Late November's floribunda blooms
lure me with crimson lips that kiss the autumn air.
How beautiful, the setting of this earth.
How profoundly sobering that it does not care
if I live, if I die.
Still, these bright blooms beckon me
to enter the silk-wall chambers of their rooms,
to linger like a sated bee, drunk with the chill of death—
autumn's destiny for all loveliness.
Time to go to bed, time to sleep, to mourn with Demeter
as she weeps for her lost daughter.
Some have asked me: "Why poetry?"
"Why not work or religion?"
"Why not make the decision to give myself over
to the good of social order?"
Poetry, I say, is choice: like love, like art, like a will that is free.
The questions may be important, but so
are the answers that come to me
through living, through breathing,
through my willingness to feed
my hungry soul poetry, so willing to eat
the words that go in, the words
that come out of me.
Like the blood-red blooms on a floribunda bush,
like the copper-colored leaves falling from oak trees
into crisp piles that look like death that looks like sleep,

leaving me to chase these words, borrowed wonder,
scattered by autumn's breath.
These dreams that tear my soul asunder,
causing me to confess new truths
that rumble like thunder in my chest,
the sound of my heart breaking for joy,
for love of this world.

Universe of Words

I am a man
in a universe
of words
looking for
the right ones
to build a place
that I might live
authentically—
if not happily—
ever after.

Word Shine

I know what it is to write,
to be committed to words,
the way one is committed to the body,
its feeding
its sex
its breathing.
Shaping the words on the tongue's
fleshy bed,
chasing the images in the letters
that thread together the beauty
I long to put into words,
the truth I dread whenever it gets
too close to the starfire chamber of my heart.
I know what it is to be driven by lexicon and diction
to find just the right syllable to create
the necessary sound for this perfect art.
This Chinese box questing, this Russian doll nesting
of meanings that are whole—
of poems, that are mirror parts
letting us see our souls in the dark
hiding from the light that these words might shine.

Reclamation

At sixty-four, the words cock and cunt
no longer overpower me—
Don't get me wrong. They have not lost
all their mystery, their allure,
their promises of pleasure, broken or not.
It's their control I've wrested from
them. Their ability to cow my will,
corral my mind with the rodeos of their
riding, lassoing, hog tying
my soul while my body writhed in the wet, dark mud of lust.
They are just words now—that and nothing more—
except for the meanings of their metaphors:
a v-shaped sheath, tailor-made for the sword,
snug as a bug in a rug, a finger in a ring, the stopper in the
silver mouth of the tub that holds
everything naked as the truth
about us:
our bodies, our souls, our need to sing
of coming together, alone,
finally at home with the power of being.

For the Love of God

To those who would make God their own,
I say, vain glory as the summer storm
that beats the coast with wind and wave.
Human words have no authority to create.
Human precepts no ability to save.
No priest or prelate, presbyter or sage,
no pope or pastor, no shaman who takes the stage
can do more than strut an idle hour.
No witch or magician, no monk or prophet
has the power to pull God's will,
like a rabbit magically conjured
out the top of a black silk hat.
No book or tablet, no scroll, no icon, or star
can reveal the perfect secret
of God's hidden, absolute heart.
All human efforts to control, to contain
are no more than shots in the dark.
All are mere dreams of the mind's sleepy schemes
trying over time to awake.
All are the cause of the shame and the pain—
the lives that we ruin, the hearts that we break
in this game that we call love of God.

Second Chances

Sometimes a second chance comes
wrapped in an unexpected smile,
in seeing a face in the sudden light of love,
as if someone turned on the switch
and in your heart, you knew you were home.
Sometimes a second chance is a simple yes
singing sweet aria above a sea of no's,
a life-vest tossed upon the waves,
a pair of arms that lift you up,
that save you from the past's cruel storms.
Sometimes a second chance is the first time
love stops you in your tracks,
takes your face in its hands,
quells the longing in your heart,
shows you how to look forward without looking back.
Sometimes a second chance is the love of your life,
the missing piece your heart couldn't find
until time, in its mercy, opened the door,
and your heart in its wisdom knew for sure
it had found its true love, and forevermore
would believe in second chances.

Night Talk

How I talk myself
into, out of being
when I leave my bed
late in the night,
unable to sleep
for the words, words, words
that keep me awake,
the images that want
to come out and play
in these letters
on these lines—
my soul on a string,
the string in a hand
of one running, running, running
to find the wind
to lift me up
to let me fly
back to the place
to begin again
to find that grace
that used to keep me company,
that made me feel whole,
that made me feel free enough
to love and to believe
that I would be loved in return.

Who Loves the Poet?

No one loves the poet.
Oh, they may sing the poet's song
and may praise the poet's words.
They may embrace the poet's insights
and viewpoint of the world.
They might teach the poet's canon
as part of curricula in schools
and romanticize the poet's legacy,
how the poet kept or broke the rules.
They might claim the poet can change the world,
might celebrate the poet's pen,
might be the poet's greatest herald,
might imagine they are the poet's best friend.
But no one loves the poet of flesh and bone—
the person who never stops questioning,
the reactionary who can never leave the status quo alone.
No one loves the poet's blood shed for beauty
until it floods the plain of truth.
No one loves the poet's mind,
that vision that sees right through the veneer
that makes believe we shine.
No one loves the poet's ear that hears hypocrisy
or the poet's temperament that elaborates the
cracks and flaws in our morality.
No one loves the poet's finger that probes the wound
below the scar until it bleeds its truth.

P.C. Scheponik

No one loves the poet, though they love what
the poet can do with words that can be bound
in books, in pages, in lines, that can be found and celebrated,
then put away like something to be
treasured, like someone to be loved—
leaving the weathered heart to its loneliness,
for the poet of flesh and blood.

"What Can I do?"

My father-in-law would ask this question often
in his early 90s when he could really do nothing.
Nonetheless, he asked it repeatedly, almost as if
he did not realize he was too unsteady on his feet,
from age and illness, too weak to even walk without
the walker—sometimes, too weak to lift the glass to
his lips to drink, or the fork to his mouth to eat.
Yet he wanted to know what he could do—as if being
was doing nothing, as if having lived ninety-one years
was not doing enough.
Sometimes I would get annoyed with him for asking the
question—especially when I was overwhelmed with
helping him to be: getting him dressed, helping him in or
out of bed, or getting him to the toilet on time.
Now, years after he is gone, now that I am retired and my
profession has been lifted off my back the way the yolk,
field harness, and the weight of the plow are taken off the
mule set out to final pasture, now that the curvature from
my lifetime of labor has formed its
permanent groove in me—
an emptiness where something heavy had been asks the
question, almost rhetorically,
"What can I do?"

For Love of Women

I never understood the misogynistic need to dominate,
through word and deed, all aspects of the feminine.
Maybe this impulse to overpower is woven into the fabric
of our being, on the most fundamental level of the
alleles—dominant vs. recessive freeing the microscopic
fist that will grow into the physical punch,
or the chromosomal penis that will one day become
the rape.
I never understood the ritual of boys who made it
a rite of passage to hate the girls: cootie calls,
long before they would transform into booty calls.
I couldn't wrap my mind around men who felt
women's primary function was getting guys laid,
and that men's duty as males was to fuck and taste
every flower in the garden.
Sex was never a competition to me.
I shied away from sports but not from knowledge
or the mystery of what I was not.
Maybe because I was raised with sisters.
From the start, I saw women differently.
Or maybe the women in my life never played
the victim.
Whatever the reason, my opinion of females
was always high, and, for me, it was never open season
on feminine wiles, neither in my body nor in my mind.
If anything, I found their charm and their allure

each a playful tease, which, more often than not,
made me the butt of jokes and a target for those
who would seize any opportunity to mock and to beat
down the enemy to crotch size.
So instead of learning to hate the feminine,
I learned to despise the brutality of my own kind—
the Y, that X missing one leg.
Maybe it isn't the missing penis that is envy's source,
but the long, lost egg.
I'm not sure if this poem is about protest
or natural selection's mistake.
All I know is I never hated women.

Sexual Persuasions

I was amazed when I first heard of a species of ant
that was all female—an Amazonian sisterhood
who thrived in the plenty of a regimented feminine
harmony. Each sister knew her place. Each tiny Amazon
lived in a male-less state, without incident, without debate—
a testament to the power of the goddess.
Then I learned of other anomalies—astounding peculiarities
surrounding the sexualities of numerous animal species.
Sexual realities that would rattle the mind, the mores,
the taboos of every kind.
Manifestations to challenge the theories of biology
and render mute the contentions of theology.
It was a sexual mythology to give worldview a pause.
There are some seventy species in all with parthenogenetic
proclivities endowed with genetic monotonies to challenge
cultural preconceptions of natural law.
There are celibate celebrities who replicate and recombine
rather than copulate at cyclic times.
Komodo dragons, hammerhead sharks, and snakes
of the species brahminy blind have perfected the art of
virgin birth.
Blue streak cleaner wrasse and clown fish can transform
their sex from female to male.
Female market squid can avoid male advances by flashing
false testes and taking their chances that they will successfully
hide their true natures from aroused males' eyes.

SEEING, BELIEVING, AND OTHER THINGS

Cuttlefish can completely divide themselves in two
creating both a male and a female side to confuse
other males trying to find mates to service their needs.
Another strange practitioner, the garter snake, the he
becomes a she, to escape a predator or to give itself
a chance to fully wake when rising from hibernation.
The hyena has a secret reason to laugh:
telling she from he is a challenging task with her
pseudo-penis and scrotal sack.
Differentiating the sexes, so elegantly masked
can baffle love's pursuit and block arousal's path.
Parrotfish are hermaphrodites who can change
their sex when conditions are right.
Moving from male to female, gender takes flight,
fluid as the waves.
With such as these in nature's plan
who is woman, who is man forms a pair of questions
like a pair of chromosomes able to expand infinitely
to meet survival's needs.

Choice Is a Solemn Matter

When I heard it was by his own hand
that he took the pills,
swallowed all of them,
cancelled his plans to attend the party,
called a friend—
so he wouldn't die alone—
I was sad, but I understood his choice
to leave.
He had beaten cancer,
but the doctors told him there was
nothing more they could do to help
him breathe.
He had just lost the mother
who had always accepted him—
a gay man's best friend.
His heart, broken in places
he couldn't reach—
wouldn't heal, couldn't deal.
He was like the succulents he grew—
in love with the sun,
at home in the desert,
where love, like water, was hard to come by.
His life always was a fight to survive.
He drove his roots deep,
found a way to thrive in a winter world
that turned a cold shoulder toward his kind.

SEEING, BELIEVING, AND OTHER THINGS

For more than fifty years he bloomed,
his flowers the type that could make you weep,
the sharp edges of his spines the only way
he could keep himself safe in this world
of natural selection with its predilection to decide
who is fit enough to stay.

Underdog

I've always been drawn to the underdog,
the odd duck, the one no one wanted on the team,
the fatty, the fruity, the one with the screw loosely in.
I sympathize with the addict, have an
ache in my heart for the homeless,
feel at home with the defeated, by self
or society, by coke or by gin.
I've a soft spot for the broken, feel a connection close as kin.
Something in me stirs for their pathos—
the fact that so many were taught how to end
before they ever learned how to begin.
I've learned their gardens of thorns,
red with blood rather than roses.
I've watched them weep and wither
and wondered if God knows how deep
their sorrow goes—
rooted in darkness, tangled in pain.
What will their harvest look like—
no water, no rain.
What will be left but dry, sharp thorns,
twisted into patterns that can never explain
the truth inside their loss.
What can be done with this but to form a crown
to place on the head of a God willing to come down
to settle the score on suffering and its portions—
how some receive so little, and some so
much more than they deserve.

Ascension

Every day he is there at the top of the stairs,
tucked in the corner to the right, asleep in the chair.
Legs crossed, head drooped, his beard
buried in his stained coat.
An open book resting upon his lap, his
hands collapsed upon the pages.
Relieved to have let go the heavy burden
of living with no particular place
to call home.
The warmth of the library during winter.
The air-conditioned cool in the summer.
He makes me think of libraries and their purpose—
a gathering place to learn to grow,
to be a mark of intellect and culture,
a place free from the tyrannies of life.
The only rule—silence.
How fortunate for him. How revealing for me.
We both come here to set ourselves free
from the world outside the library's doors.
Each of us with different circumstances,
both of us wanting more than what the working world
offers.
I feel my condescension melting, my heart growing softer.
We are brothers in spirit and need inside these walls that offer
safety and solitude to a pair of wanderers
looking to keep going
in a world more than willing to stop us.

Old Men and Their Dogs

I see us every morning—
old men and our dogs,
out for our constitutionals.
The remains of manhood
walking love on a leash—
maybe obedience, control at least.
Each of us an aged Ulysses who leaves
the comfort of fireplace and friends
to ford out each sunrise
like white-haired wayfarers
before the odyssey ends.
Our hands clutching something taut,
still able to feel the pull of importance—
even if it's just pretend.
How we stop at every hydrant
and island of weeds for our first mates
to pee—
how we carefully bend to bag life's debris
left behind.
The way we were by time's cruel inclemency—
worse than the women who could turn us
into pigs,
far worse than the giants with their single
hungry eyes,
devouring our lives, no matter how we prayed,
no matter how we tried.

SEEING, BELIEVING, AND OTHER THINGS

How do we fight a witch, a giant, or a god
when each of us is just a man with
a dream, and a fifty-year plan
that is no more.
So we give a call or a whistle,
jingle the leash, open the door
and sail off into the sunrise before
the day's aches and pains makes us too sore.
Lead in hand, pup out ahead—
one foot after the other—
still sure we can find our way home,
so thankful we are not dead,
each day growing slower,
the world growing colder
with each step.

Poem Almost Never Written

You were almost the poem never written,
the blank page I somehow forgot.
Your lines lying empty, hungry for words—
a vacancy living between pages already versed.
How blank, how void your world must have been
without the love of language, unkissed by the pen.
Were you famished for letters? Did you thirst for ink?
Did the vacuum of your space give you pause to think?
Or were you nonexistent like the world between blinks.
I am here. You are saved, lettered to life this day.
I baptize your empty lines with words
that give you something to say
to a world that might be listening.

Butterfly Boy

This is a story of a boy who became a man
who tried to become a boy again.
It wasn't for lack of love, need for sex
that the man longed.
Rather it was love of innocence lost
that struck the spark
that smoldered into flames,
which consumed the forest of his heart
till not a single tree remained.
And the man at last could clearly see
good and evil and the difference between.
How he wanted to find his way back to the boy
who would chase butterflies in the field—
play catch and release with their powdery wings
in a world so real with beauty, with truth of sun and sky.
He was so young, so free. He was so alive.
It was a time of personal Pangea,
when his heart and soul were one.
It was a time of perfect unity,
when he did not need to become
anything more than the child he was—
so wrought with feelings, with life, so in love.
The boy who finally remembered himself,
running freely in the fields of the old man's mind.

The Past Cannot Live Up to Itself

What is it that makes me hunger for the past, the
need to return to my childhood home—
402 Blue Buff Road. Somehow the house seems
too small for the memories that live there.
Maybe, like Alice, I need to drink something to
make me smaller, or eat something to make me
taller. Maybe the past is the rabbit hole and memories
are like members at the tea party—some,
like the rabbit, too late—having missed the important
date. Others are mad as hatters for what
they did or did not do— or for what's been done to
them. Still others are like the Queen of Hearts
screaming wildly, "Off with their heads!" Decapitation
being the only way to stop the pen, put
the dead to rest. Still, the call to go back is strong,
and the journey never as good as the stories
memory tells—little white lies trying to hide larger,
darker truths, make them disappear like the
Cheshire Cat, but the mind can grin so much
deeper than darkness. I can never be more than
an interloper from another time when I return to the
past—sneak in through a window if the doors
are locked—as they so often are. And I never really
find what I'm looking for—that missing key
that opens the room where the mystery is hidden.
Yet I keep trying—bidden or unbidden.
The force to go back is driving me home to where
the heart once was— before I ever lost it.

Poet

He was a young boy,
alone,
so different from all the others.
He was unamerican—
didn't like baseball,
didn't want to run the bases with the gang
in the schoolyard or on the raked diamond field.
He didn't want to slay the dragon.
He saw the beauty in its enameled scales
and found a certain truth in the feel of breathing fire.
His was not a world of trucks and fists.
His was a jungle of desires wrapped around his heart,
tangled up in his soul.
His mind was the machete he used
to cut through the deep roots of feelings,
that released the blood that became the ink
of his salvation—
his link to life, to sanity, to belief that the world
belonged to him, too,
that there was a place for boys who chased butterflies,
who cried over sunsets, who listened to the sea,
who mourned the waning moon.
His would be a different kind of life—
one lived in journals through pens—
the best of him remembered in words, his friends,
who would teach him who he was.

Pain Deep

January breathes icy sighs this morning.
Sea oats, diamond-coated with last night's
dusting of snow, shiver in the morning cold.
Sea grass pokes through the snow-capped dunes,
and the beach is a river of ice milk strewn
with footprints of hurried pipers and hungry gulls.
Above, the sky, the color of battleship hulls,
broods like a bearer of bad news.
The morning is a marriage of grey and white moods,
a scene where silence rules,
save the scratchy rasps of tumbling leaves
as they grasp the sides of curb, trying to keep
from blowing too far from the limbs of the trees
they once called home.
It is a morning when the only one pleased
is Winter who owns the world for a season.
Persephone's rape still gives Demeter a reason
to take all hope, all warmth away,
leaving only white whispers of memories to say
how deep a mother's pain can be.

Love's Tabernacle

We were once young and beautiful.
Passion was our every thought.
Desire, the bounty of our bodies,
the pleasured touch of being entwined,
the rapid breaths, the raging rush of blood
to all those sacred places where we made
fire that burned like love.
We were all to each other
as the stars above are all to the night.
How we lay in the after-glow of the love
we made.
The tiny fires in our flesh, radiant embers
after the blaze.
Your palm upon my heaving chest,
my fingertips tracing the curve of your face.
All was satiation. All was grace,
in the tabernacle of our love.

Youth's Season

What is there in age,
but the memory of youth's beauty,
the promises the body made
and broke with the passage of the years.
What remains are fond thoughts of freedom
when strength and desire had their fair share
of who we were when faces were free of
traces of worry that wore grooves like tiny
tributaries round eyes and mouths,
made furrows in the once smooth terrain
of brows.
When skin was taut and muscles firm.
When we took risks and hadn't yet learned
that youth would not be ours forever.
When love was wild and without bounds.
When we were free and responsibility
had not yet found our hiding places.
When our feelings were sacraments
and our bodies the only source of grace
we needed.
Till age took us by the hand, and wisdom
pleaded that we understand,
and we reasoned we were lucky to have
ever had the chance to enjoy youth's
precious season.

What to Say (For Heather Harris)

What can I say to the one who lost her father,
her hero, her protector, her friend.
The one she looked up to.
The one, who, in the end, became the child she cared for.
What is there in heaven or prayer to comfort her
after all the years of suffering.
There was no cure but death to relieve him from his pain—
to give her back her life again.
But to what purpose—
the caregiving having hollowed out a great hole
in her life, in her soul.
What can I tell her that will console
her empty heart.
"You will see him again," seems a Christmas
wish list.
"Time will heal," seems rather trite.
Maybe I should just be honest—
tell her she lived her life like so many of us,
believing the lie that love could make everything
better.
Certainly, not her father.
Certainly, she loved
to the point of bathing and feeding him,
of sleeping by his side, of listening to
his labored breathing, of willing with her
entire being the breath her father couldn't seem to catch,

P.C. Scheponik

to the point of reading to him, of holding
his hand, of watching his veins grow thin
as the tubes that ran like small plastic rivers
from the oxygen tank to his nose.
Certainly, love would not save her from the
burden she bore, from the deep sense of loss
she would come to know when her father died.
Maybe the best thing I could do was to say
nothing. Just be there to hand her the tissues
when she cried.
To give her a hug and tell her I didn't know why
we must suffer and still have to say goodbye.
To tell her the stars have no answers, and
the sun and moon, for all their light, will never
tell us why.
To tell her our own heart is all that anyone
ever really has, and the best we can do is to hold
it gently when it breaks.

Loving My Father

It's much easier loving my father since his death.
I can choose the good things to remember—
forget how we couldn't be in the same room together,
how he could crush me with a look,
how his strength was more condemnation than protection.
I couldn't be the fighter he wanted,
couldn't stand up to the bullies—
how I caught a ball like a girl—
though I wasn't, never wanted to be,
how I liked stuffed animals more than trucks and toy guns.
I grew up on the disapproval I felt—
whether true or not, it was too true for me.
I only wanted to run away, to find a place
where I could be safe being me.
I loved words and color, sunsets, stars, and leaves.
Each time I saw a bird take to wing,
I knew I was born to be free.
I loved the flow of sheets in the wind and the swirling
cascade of streams.
But I was a 50's son, and the world was not ready for me.
I don't blame my father for who he was any more than I
blame myself for who I am.
If there is any blame to be assigned, it belongs to our inability
to understand who we are and why we bleed so readily at
another's touch.
Now that my father is gone, there is

much I can find to remember
in love—
how he finally let go and let me grow into myself,
how I learned he loved the man in me, though he
could never reach the boy,
how he stood at the foot of my hospital bed,
willing me to be well,
rubbing my feet as if to press the stroke away,
catching the bits and pieces of me,
molding them into something that could be whole—
a tabernacle of love where I could let my soul heal,
where I could make love real, love for my father
that would last me the rest of my life.

The Grieving

Thirteen years have passed since I lost him,
my father,
who left this world with a single deep grunt—
as if his soul backed up, charged the door
that was his body and broke through into
eternity,
leaving the hulking physical shell of himself
behind on the bed,
like a giant chrysalis, emptied.
Just the husk of who he was lying there
in physical ruination.
As if life said, "I am done. I'm outta here!"
I never heard my father leave.
I never saw his body on the bedroom bed—
inanimate as the sheets and comforter,
the dresser, four walls, the bedroom door,
ajar like a gaping mouth.
I was at work in my office between lectures
when I got the call from my brother-in-law
telling me to come to St. Luke's Hospital.
The moment he said, "Your father… ,"
I knew that Dad was dead.
I cannot—even now—explain the hollowness
I became,
as if someone had pierced my body's skin with
a mystical straw and sucked the soul right out of me.

I fled my office, running away from death but
toward my father's body without hope, without breath.
When I got to the emergency room, found his lifeless
form—all that was left
was for me to tell him how much I loved him still—
the rest was leaning on the hospital litter that held him
and the sobs that punched their way out of my heaving chest.
You would think that after thirteen years I wouldn't still be
writing about his death.
What is the lifespan of grief?
Though we do our best to go on,
what is the expiration date for the warranty of love
between a father and a son?
Some questions have no answers.

Efficiency

I lie awake in the small dark night of my
mother's efficiency apartment.
She has been ill, and I have come to
make sure that she is not alone.
She sleeps in the full bed, curled to one side.
The rest of the bed, a yawn of space, an
empty place where the memory
of my father might lie down.
It has been thirteen years since his death—
thirteen years for my mother to build
an efficiency of emptiness—
photos on coffee and end tables, on the refrigerator's side,
in a large frame above the TV—
the ways my mother hides from
death, holds on to the life left
to her through memories she fears she
might lose to illness, to age.
I see the rosary I gave her, lying in a silent pile of beads,
waiting for her fingertips to roll them into prayers that plead
for the relief of death to free her from her sorrow, to give her
the chance for a tomorrow where she
might see, again, her husband
of sixty-two years, her parents, her
brothers, her grandson, lost too
soon, her friends that death has taken
away, left her alone in this

efficiency room, like a loose end to be tied up—
sooner she prays rather than later.
I lie awake, a son who can do nothing to make things better
for the mother he loves.
I think my heart is breaking—
there is too much taking in this world,
not enough giving—
Oh, the loving! Oh, the living! Oh, how
we are driven by our tears.

Blame Game

I've always felt there's more sorrow in me
than I've earned through thought or deed.
My mind is divided into two great ravines:
one of guilt, the other of grief
carved by rivers of sorrow and shame.
What have I done to merit such misery,
to deserve such psychic pain?
The torturer and tortured are one and the same
in the dungeon of my mind,
in the dark and derelict game I play
where I seek until I find the blame
and create a reason to make it mine.

Photo by Melissa Diliberto.

About the Author

P.C. Scheponik began writing poetry at nine years old. At thirteen, he had his first poetry publication in a local newspaper. His poems celebrate the beauty and brutality of nature, explore the passions, pleasures, and pains of being human, analyze the complexities of familial love, and contemplate the challenges and wonders of the metaphysical mysteries of life. He taught composition and poetry at Montgomery County Community College. He has published four collections of poems: *Psalms to Padre Pio* (National Centre for Padre Pio, INC), *A Storm by Any Other Name* and *Songs the Sea has Sung in Me* (PS Books, a division of Philadelphia Stories), and *And the Sun Still Dared to Shine* (Mazo Publishers). His work has also appeared in numerous literary journals. He is a 2019 *Pushcart Prize* nominee. His newest collection is Seeing, Believing, and Other Things, published by *Adelaide Books*. Since retiring, he resides with his wife, Shirley, and their shizon, Bella in a small condo by the sea. There the beauty of the natural surroundings offers a continual source of joy and inspiration to fuel his writing.

www.ingramcontent.com/pod-product-compliance
Lightning Source LLC
Chambersburg PA
CBHW071414070526
44578CB00003B/577